THE **ROTISSERIE CHICKEN** COOKBOOK

TARRAGON CHICKEN SALAD STUFFED
CHERRY TOMATOES, 14

MONTE CRISTO MINIS, 37

CHICKEN AND KOHLRABI SOUP, 84

BOMBAY TOMATO-CHICKEN SOUP, 48

CHICKEN AND ESCAROLE SOUP, 68

CHICKEN, WILD RICE, AND MUSHROOM
SOUP, 72

CREAMY CHICKEN AND PEA SALAD, 86

AVOCADO-CHICKEN SALAD WITH MELONS AND HONEY MUSTARD DRESSING, 87

BBQ CHICKEN SALAD WITH CORN BREAD CROUTONS, 94

CHICKEN SALAD WITH PEAR AND GORGONZOLA DRESSING, 108

REUBEN-STYLE CHICKEN SANDWICHES WITH SPECIAL SAUCE, 114

CHICKEN FLORENTINE SANDWICHES, 117

PHILLY CHEESE CHICKEN SANDWICHES, 122

GREEK CHICKEN PITAS, 133

PRONTO CHICKEN MARSALA, 145

MINUTE STROGANOFF WITH
CHICKEN, 183

CHICKEN PARMESAN CALZONE, 146

CHICKEN FETTUCCINE WITH WALNUTS,
CRANBERRIES, AND ARUGULA, 153

PRESTO PESTO CHICKEN PENNE, 171

ROSEMARY CHICKEN AND CHEVRE
STUFFED PORTABELLAS, 144

CHICKEN-ARTICHOKE CASSEROLE, 186

CURRIED CHICKEN CASSEROLE, 188

QUICK CHICKEN DIVAN, 199

CHICKEN AND ASPARAGUS CRÊPES, 222

CRUSTLESS CHICKEN BROCCOLI-CHEDDAR QUICHE, 226

CHICKEN QUICHE MEDITERRANEAN, 232

BREAKFAST TURNOVERS, 233

TARRAGON CHICKEN OMELET WITH HAVARTI, 236

CHICKEN AND GRITS CASSEROLE, 237

CHICKEN ARTICHOKE FRITTATA, 238

THE

ROTISSERIE CHICKEN

COOKBOOK

THE
ROTISSERIE CHICKEN
COOKBOOK

Home-Made Meals with Store-Bought Convenience

MICHELLE ANN ANDERSON

CUMBERLAND HOUSE
NASHVILLE, TENNESSEE

The Rotisserie Chicken Cookbook
Published by Cumberland House Publishing, Inc.
431 Harding Industrial Drive
Nashville, TN 37211-3160

Cover design: JulesRulesDesign
Text design: Julie Pitkin

ISBN-13: 978-1-60751-368-1

Printed in the United States of America

For Chuck and Jordan,
my biggest cheerleaders:
Thanks for all your love and support…we did it!

CONTENTS

INTRODUCTION

I love cooking…always have. As a little girl growing up in the 70s, one of my most treasured "toys" was my Easy Bake Oven™. I spent many busy hours with that thing. Once the little prepackaged mixes ran out, though, I had to get creative in order to keep cooking. That challenge fueled my creativity in the kitchen and really was the beginning of what has become an exciting and fulfilling lifelong joy of cooking.

While I have fun being imaginative while cooking, life as a busy mom often leaves little time for much culinary experimentation. Like many hectic home cooks, I've come to rely on some convenience foods to help me get dinner on the table. One ingredient that has become a staple in our home is the rotisserie chicken. Talk about a time saver! They really do help me to focus on the part of cooking I enjoy most—trying new and interesting flavor combinations.

The rotisserie chickens I find in my local market are about 24 ounces. This size bird yields an average of 4 cups of white meat and 2 cups dark. I have found that separating the meat from bone is easiest after letting the chicken cool just long enough so that I can handle it with my bare hands without getting burned. Then, I just use my fingers to pull the chicken meat off the bone. For recipes that call for carving the bird into parts, a sharp pair of kitchen shears and a small boning knife are my tools of choice. I first remove the silicone band or plastic parts holding the legs and/or wings. Start with the drumsticks by pulling them up to locate the joint, and cut them off using the knife. I tackle the wings and thighs by carving them out with the knife. Again, pulling them to help me to locate the joint. The shears are useful for cutting the breasts. Starting at the bottom cavity, with the shears just slightly off center of the breast bone, cut towards the neck. Then, cut down the back, to cut the breast loose. Some recipes utilize sliced breast meat. Start at either end of the breast, carving with the boning knife at an angle to cut the meat away from the ribs. For slicing, I prefer to wait until after the meat has chilled in the refrigerator for at least 30 minutes. This helps to end up with very thin slices.

Many of the recipes in this book call for chicken broth. There are many good quality broths available now. One word of caution, though. Some can be a bit salty. I recommend purchasing low-sodium varieties whenever possible.

Having said that, though, homemade broth is so easy to make. I take all the bones and skin left after carving and toss them into a large, lidded plastic container housed in my freezer. Any pieces of vegetables and herbs (stems and all) left after peeling and cutting are added as well. After I've accumulated quite a bit, they all get tossed into my crock pot. Depending on the mix of vegetables that have collected, the addition of fresh carrots, onions and celery may be in order. Pour in enough water to cover, toss in a bay leaf or two and a sprinkling of peppercorns, turn the heat on to high and walk away. Eight hours later, a flavorful broth is born. After it's cooled, simply strain and pour into freezer containers and freeze for use in your favorite recipes.

Speaking of recipes, you'll find quite a varied collection here. From traditional recipes reconstructed to make them easier like the Pronto Chicken Marsala and Minute Stroganoff with Chicken, to those containing flavors used in unexpected ways like Tarragon Chicken Omelet with Havarti, Green Curry Chicken Potstickers and Chicken Florentine Sandwiches, the one common thread is the use of rotisserie chicken. So, swing by the market and pick one up, and see how delicious fast food can be.

Happy Cooking!

APPETIZERS

Brie, Cranberry, and Chicken Mini Pizzas

Pizza never had it so good…the twang of cranberry pairs perfectly with the creamy Brie melting deliciously over the chicken.

½	cup whole berry cranberry sauce
1	teaspoon finely chopped fresh basil
½	teaspoon finely chopped fresh rosemary
½	teaspoon minced roasted garlic
6	frozen dinner roll dough pieces, thawed
½	cup cubed rotisserie chicken
2	ounces Brie cheese, sliced
6	teaspoons shredded Parmesan cheese
1	tablespoon finely snipped fresh chives

Step 1: PREHEAT OVEN AND PREPARE PAN

Preheat the oven to 350° F. Spray a baking sheet with cooking spray.

Step 2: MAKE SAUCE

Stir together the cranberry sauce, basil, rosemary, and garlic in a small bowl. Set aside.

Step 3: SHAPE PIZZAS

Press each dough ball flat into the shape of a pizza. Arrange 2 inches apart on the prepared baking sheet.

Step 4: ASSEMBLE AND BAKE

Spread 1 heaping tablespoon of herbed cranberry sauce over the pizza crust to within ¼ inch of the edge. Top with even amounts of chicken and Brie. Sprinkle with Parmesan. Bake in the preheated oven for 20 minutes or until the crust is golden and the cheese is melted.

Step 5: GARNISH AND SERVE

Sprinkle each pizza with fresh chives. Serve hot.

COOKS NOTES: On its own, this mini pizza makes a perfect appetizer. Served with a salad, it's a terrific lunch or light dinner.

• MAKES 6 SERVINGS •

Chicken and Brie Tarts with Fig

With only 5 ingredients, these little gems practically make themselves!

½	cup diced rotisserie chicken
⅓	cup prepared fig jam
15	½-inch cubes Brie cheese
1	2.1-ounce package frozen pre-baked filo shells
	A few chives, finely chopped for garnish

Step 1: PREHEAT OVEN AND PREPARE TARTS

Preheat the oven to 350° F. Arrange filo shells on an ungreased baking sheet. Set aside.

Step 2: FILL TARTS

Place a heaping teaspoon of chicken into each filo shell, followed by a teaspoon of jam. Place a slice of Brie on top.

Step 3: BAKE, GARNISH, AND SERVE

Bake the filled tarts in the preheated oven for 12 to 15 minutes, or until the cheese is melted and bubbly. Place the tarts on serving platter, sprinkle with chives, and serve.

COOKS NOTES: Apricot preserves are a delicious substitution for the fig jam.

• MAKES 4-6 SERVINGS •

Tarragon Chicken Salad Stuffed Cherry Tomatoes

Tarragon and bacon really dress up this chicken salad.

2	cups diced rotisserie chicken
1	tablespoon prepared bacon pieces
½	cup mayonnaise
2	green onions, sliced thin
2	tablespoons chopped flat leaf parsley
1	tablespoon chopped fresh tarragon leaves
	Kosher salt to taste
	Ground black pepper to taste
2	dozen cherry tomatoes

Step 1: MAKE SALAD FILLING

In a medium bowl, stir together the chicken, bacon, mayonnaise, onion, parsley, tarragon, salt and pepper. Cover and refrigerate for at least an hour to overnight.

Step 2: PREPARE TOMATOES

Cut off a small slice of the bottom of each tomato to keep it from rolling. Slice the stem end off of each tomato. Scoop out and discard the flesh of each tomato. Set aside.

Step 3: ASSEMBLE AND SERVE

Fill each tomato with the chicken salad mixture. Arrange on a serving platter. Serve cold.

COOKS NOTES: Basil works well in place of the tarragon.

• MAKES 6-8 SERVINGS •

Chicken Mole Empanadas

Just the right amount of spice in these little bites.

1	cup diced rotisserie chicken
½	cup prepared mole
½	cup loosely packed cilantro, chopped
12	each frozen dinner roll dough balls, thawed
1	egg, beaten
1	tablespoon milk

Step 1: PREHEAT OVEN AND PREPARE PAN

Preheat the oven to 350° F. Spray a baking sheet with cooking spray. Set aside.

Step 2: MAKE FILLING

Mix together the chicken, mole, and cilantro in a small bowl.

Step 3: ASSEMBLE EMPANADAS

On a floured work surface, roll out a dinner roll dough ball in to a circle, about ¼-inch thick. Place a heaping tablespoon of the filling in the center of the dough. Fold in half, crimping the edges together with a fork to seal well. Continue assembling with the remaining ingredients.

Step 4: BAKE

Arrange the assembled empanadas 3 inches apart on the prepared baking sheet. Mix together the egg and milk in a small bowl. Brush over the empanadas. Bake in the pre-heated oven for 15 to 20 minutes or until golden. Serve warm.

• MAKES 4-6 SERVINGS •

Sweet Pepper Relleno Poppers

Miniature sweet peppers filled with chicken and pepper jack cheese make terrific appetizers or party hors d'oeuvres.

16	to 20 small sweet peppers, red, yellow and/or orange
½	cup finely diced rotisserie chicken
½	8-ounce container chive and onion-flavored cream cheese, softened
½	cup shredded pepper jack cheese
2	green onions, sliced, divided
1	tablespoon chopped cilantro leaves
1	egg
¼	cup milk
1	cup corn masa flour
1	cup panko (Japanese bread crumbs)
	Canola oil for frying
	Kosher salt
1	green pepper, sliced
½	cup prepared jalapeño jelly, warmed

Step 1: **PREPARE PEPPERS**

Place the peppers in a microwave safe dish; cook on high for 1 to 2 minutes, or until the peppers are slightly softened. Cool to room temperature. Make a slit on one side of each pepper. Gently reach into the pepper and remove the seeds and membrane. Leave the stems on.

Step 2: **MAKE FILLING**

Mix together the chicken, cream cheese, pepper jack cheese, 1 green onion, and cilantro in a small bowl.

Step 2: **STUFF PEPPERS**

With a small spoon, gently fill the peppers with the chicken mixture. Set aside.

Step 3: **SET UP BREADING STATION**

In a shallow dish, beat together the egg and milk. Mix together the corn masa flour and panko in a second shallow dish.

Step 4: BREAD PEPPERS

Dip the peppers in the egg and milk mixture. Then, dip in the panko mixture, taking care to cover the entire pepper. Set aside.

Step 5: FRY PEPPERS

Pour the oil to a depth of 4 inches in a large Dutch oven over medium high. When the oil reaches 350° F, gently place 6 to 8 of the peppers into the oil and fry, turning occasionally, until golden and crisp. Continue to fry in batches of 6 to 8 peppers. Drain on a paper towel-lined plate. Sprinkle with salt and pepper while hot.

Step 6: GARNISH AND SERVE

Arrange the peppers on a serving platter; sprinkle with the remaining green onion. Serve with warmed jalapeño jelly for dipping.

• MAKES 8-10 SERVINGS •

Green Curry Chicken Potstickers with Dipping Sauce

Traditional potstickers infused with Thai flavors.

½	cup diced rotisserie chicken
½	teaspoon green curry paste
½	cup fresh baby spinach, chopped
¼	cup shredded carrot
2	green onions, sliced, divided
½	cup coconut milk
	About 32 round wonton wrappers
3	tablespoons peanut oil
1	cup water
	Prepared sweet Thai chili sauce

Step 1: MAKE FILLING

Place the chicken, curry paste, spinach, carrot, onion, and coconut milk into the bowl of a food processor fitted with a metal blade. Pulse until the mixture is coarsely chopped and well blended.

Step 2: FILL POTSTICKERS

Place a tablespoon of filling in the center of a wonton wrapper. Moisten the edges with water. Fold in half, pressing well to seal the edges. Place the posticker on a parchment-lined baking sheet. Continue to assemble with the remaining ingredients.

Step 3: COOK POTSTICKERS

Pour 1 tablespoon of peanut oil into a large skillet or wok over medium high heat. When the oil is hot, carefully place about one third of the potstickers into the pan. Cook for 2 to 3 minutes, without turning, or until they begin to brown. Pour ⅓ cup of water into the skillet and cover. Reduce the heat to low and simmer for 3 to 4 minutes. Remove the potstickers to a serving platter; hold in a warm oven. Wipe out the skillet. Cook the remaining potstickers following the above cooking instructions.

Step 4: GARNISH AND SERVE

Arrange potstickers on a platter and sprinkle with the remaining green onion. Serve with sweet Thai chili sauce for dipping.

COOKS NOTES: Potstickers can be made ahead of time and frozen. Place assembled potstickers on a parchment lined baking sheet; freeze for 30 minutes or until solid. Store in freezer bags until use.

• MAKES 10-12 SERVINGS •

Buffalo Chicken Party Dip

This zesty dip comes together in no time.

1	8-ounce package cream cheese, softened
¼	cup hot pepper sauce
½	cup prepared blue cheese salad dressing
2	cups diced rotisserie chicken
1	cup shredded Monterey Jack cheese
½	cup crumbled blue cheese
6	to 8 ribs celery, cut into 3-inch lengths

Step 1: MAKE DIP

Mix together the cream cheese, pepper sauce, dressing, chicken, and Jack cheese in a medium microwave safe dish.

Step 2: HEAT DIP

Heat the dip in the microwave for 3 to 4 minutes at 70% power, or until the cheese is melted and bubbling.

Step 3: GARNISH AND SERVE

Sprinkle the dip with crumbled blue cheese, and place the dish on the center of a serving platter. Arrange celery pieces around the dip and serve.

• MAKES 4-6 SERVINGS •

Petite Chicken Croquettes
with Balsamic-Cranberry Drizzle

Miniature chicken patties with a sweet and zesty dipping sauce make for a terrific appetizer.

4	tablespoons butter, divided
1	to 2 shallots, minced
2	teaspoons minced garlic, divided
¼	cup balsamic vinegar
1	cup prepared jellied cranberry sauce
½	cup frozen diced onion, thawed and minced
1	small rib celery, minced
1	small carrot, finely grated
1½	cups finely chopped rotisserie chicken
2	tablespoons flat leaf parsley, finely chopped
2	cups seasoned bread crumbs, divided
1¼	cup milk, divided
2	eggs, divided
1	cup milk
	Canola oil for frying
	Kosher salt
1	green onion, sliced

Step 1: MAKE BALSAMIC-CRANBERRY DRIZZLE

Place 2 tablespoons of butter in a large skillet over medium high; add the shallots and cook for 3 to 4 minutes, or until translucent. Add 1 teaspoon of garlic and cook 1 minute more. Pour in the vinegar, stirring to loosen the brown bits on the bottom of the pan. Stir in the cranberry sauce. Continue to cook and stir until the sauce is melted. Reduce the temperature to low; keep warm until serving.

Step 2: COMBINE CROQUETTE INGREDIENTS

Place the remaining butter in a large skillet over medium heat. Add the onion, celery, and carrot. Cook for 3 to 4 minutes, or until the vegetables are soft. Stir in the remaining garlic and cook 1 minute longer. Remove from the heat; stir in the chicken, parsley, and ½ cup of bread crumbs. Whisk together ¼ cup of milk and 1 egg in a small bowl; stir into the chicken mixture.

Step 3: FORM CROQUETTES

Shape 2 tablespoons of the chicken mixture into a small patty. Place on a parchment paper-lined baking sheet; continue forming patties with the remaining chicken mixture. Cover and refrigerate for 1 hour. Place the remaining bread crumbs in a shallow dish; set aside. Beat together the remaining egg and milk in another shallow dish. Dip croquettes in the egg mixture, turning to coat. Dredge in bread crumbs, taking care to coat completely.

Step 4: FRY CROQUETTES

Pour the oil to a depth of 1 inch in a large skillet or Dutch oven and heat over medium high heat. When the oil reaches 350° F, gently place the croquettes into the oil and fry for 1 to 2 minutes or until golden and crisp on the bottom. Carefully turn and fry 1 to 2 minutes more, or until golden and crisp on the second side. Place on a paper towel-lined plate. Sprinkle with salt while hot.

Step 5: GARNISH AND SERVE

Arrange the croquettes on a serving platter. Decoratively spoon Balsamic-Cranberry Drizzle over the croquettes and sprinkle with green onion. Serve while hot.

• MAKES 6-8 SERVINGS •

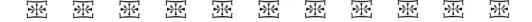

Teriyaki Chicken DIY Handrolls

For a Japanese-themed get-together, treat your guests to a fun, do-it-yourself "sushi bar."

2	cups sushi rice
2	cups water
2	tablespoons seasoned rice vinegar
2	cups shredded rotisserie chicken
¼	cup prepared teriyaki sauce
2	green onions, cut lengthwise into thirds, then into strips
1	carrot, cut into matchsticks
½	cucumber, cut into matchsticks
½	pound enoki mushrooms, cleaned and trimmed
1	avocado, diced and tossed with 1 teaspoon lemon juice
1	small bunch of cilantro
¼	cup black sesame seeds
¼	cup white sesame seeds
1	6-ounce package nori sheets

Step 1: MAKE RICE

Rinse the rice until the water runs clear. Place the rice and 2 cups of water in a medium stock pot over high heat. Bring to a boil; reduce the heat to low. Cover and cook for 20 minutes, or until the rice is tender. Remove from the heat. Stir in the vinegar. Set aside.

Step 2: SAUCE CHICKEN

Mix together the chicken and teriyaki sauce in a medium bowl. Set aside.

Step 3: ASSEMBLE SUSHI BAR

Place each ingredient i a separate serving container.

Step 4: ASSEMBLE HAND ROLLS

Hold a nori sheet in the palm of one hand. Spoon a small portion of rice onto the center of the nori. Place a spoonful of chicken over rice, followed by desired toppings. Roll into a cone shape and enjoy.

• MAKES 6-8 SERVINGS •

Mini Chicken Piroshki

From Russia with love, these little morsels are similar to Empanadas, with a twist!

3	tablespoons butter, divided
1	cup frozen diced onion
1	cup packaged angel hair shredded cabbage
1	cup diced rotisserie chicken
2	teaspoons dried dill weed
1/2	cup sour cream
	Kosher salt to taste
	Ground black pepper to taste
12	pieces frozen dinner roll dough, thawed

Step 1: PREHEAT OVEN AND PREPARE PAN

Preheat the oven to 350° F. Spray a baking sheet with cooking spray. Set aside.

Step 2: MAKE FILLING

In a large skillet over medium heat, melt 1 tablespoon of the butter. Add the onion; cook for 3 to 4 minutes, or until translucent. Stir in the cabbage; cook until just tender-crisp. Add the chicken, dill weed, and sour cream. Check the seasoning, adding salt and pepper as needed. Remove from the heat.

Step 3: ASSEMBLE PIROSHKI

On a floured work surface, roll out a dinner roll dough ball in to a circle about ¼-inch thick. Place a heaping tablespoon of the filling in the center of the dough. Fold in half, crimping the edges together with a fork to seal well. Continue with the remaining dough.

Step 4: BAKE

Arrange the assembled Piroshki 3 inches apart on the prepared baking sheet. Melt the remaining butter and brush over the Piroshki. Bake in the preheated oven for 15 to 20 minutes or until golden. Serve warm.

• MAKES 4-6 SERVINGS •

Chicken Samosas with Yogurt Dipping Sauce

Traditional Samosas are a bit time consuming; this quick adaptation is a delicious take on the classic.

2	tablespoons vegetable oil
$\frac{1}{2}$	cup frozen diced onion
$\frac{1}{2}$	cup minced rotisserie chicken
$\frac{1}{4}$	cup frozen Southern-style hash brown potatoes, thawed and minced
$\frac{1}{4}$	cup frozen peas, thawed
$\frac{1}{2}$	teaspoon minced garlic
$\frac{1}{2}$	teaspoon minced fresh ginger
$\frac{1}{4}$	teaspoon garam masala spice blend
	Several drops Tabasco Green Pepper Sauce (jalapeño flavor)
	Kosher salt
	Ground black pepper
1	teaspoon lemon juice
2	tablespoons chopped fresh cilantro leaves, divided
24	Wonton wrappers
	Canola oil for frying
$\frac{1}{2}$	cup plain yogurt
1	green onion, thinly sliced

Step 1: PREPARE FILLING

Pour the vegetable oil into a large skillet over medium heat; add the onion. Cook for 3 to 4 minutes, or until translucent. Add the chicken, potatoes, peas, garlic, ginger, garam masala, Tabasco, salt, and pepper. Cook for 3 to 5 minutes, or until heated through. Remove from the heat; stir in the lemon juice and 1 tablespoon of cilantro.

Step 2: ASSEMBLE SAMOSAS

Place a wonton wrapper on the work surface. Put a heaping tablespoon of filling onto the center of the wrapper. Moisten the edges of the wrapper with a little water. Fold in half to form a triangle, pressing the edges to seal well. Place on a parchment paper-lined baking sheet. Continue assembling with the remaining ingredients.

Step 3: FRY AND SERVE

Pour the oil to a depth of 2 inches in a large Dutch oven over medium high heat. When oil reaches 350° F, gently place samosas into the oil and fry, turning occasionally until golden and crisp. Fry in batches of 6 to 8 samosas. Drain on a paper towel lined plate. Sprinkle with salt while hot.

Step 4: GARNISH AND SERVE

Place yogurt in a small bowl and place on the center of a large platter. Arrange samosas around the yogurt bowl. Sprinkle with remaining cilantro and green onion. Serve hot.

• MAKES 6-8 SERVINGS •

Chinese Chicken Baked Buns

Reminiscent of authentic Chinese dim sum.

1	cup diced rotisserie chicken
2	tablespoons prepared hoisin sauce
2	green onions, sliced
	Flour for work surface
12	frozen dinner roll dough pieces, thawed
3	tablespoons sesame oil
2	teaspoons sesame seeds

Step 1: PREHEAT OVEN AND PREPARE PAN

Preheat the oven to 350° F. Spray baking sheet with cooking spray.

Step 2: MAKE FILLING

Stir together the chicken, hoisin sauce, and green onion in a medium bowl. Set aside.

Step 3: ASSEMBLE BUNS

On a floured work surface, flatten a dinner roll dough ball until about ¼-inch thick. Place a heaping tablespoon of the filling in the center of the dough. Fold the dough into a ball around the filling, pinching the edges together to seal well. Continue with the remaining dough.

Step 4: RISE BUNS

Arrange assembled buns 3 inches apart on the prepared baking sheet. Brush the buns with sesame oil and sprinkle with sesame seeds. Cover with a damp cloth, place in a draft free location, and let rise for 30 minutes.

Step 5: BAKE AND SERVE

Bake the buns in a 350° F preheated oven for 15 to 20 minutes, or until golden brown.

COOKS NOTES: While savory hoisin sauce can be found in the Asian section of most well-stocked markets, plum and teriyaki sauces make tasty substitutions.

• MAKES 6-8 SERVINGS•

Thai Chicken Cucumber Cups

These delightful little appetizers make a nice start to a Thai themed dinner.

1	cup shredded rotisserie chicken
1	cup cooked Jasmine rice
½	cup shredded coconut
2	tablespoons sweet Thai chili sauce
2	tablespoons finely chopped cilantro
2	tablespoons finely chopped Thai basil
1	green onion, finely sliced on the bias
	Juice of 1 lime
	Zest of 1 lime
2	to 3 large English cucumbers
2	tablespoons black sesame seeds

Step 1: MAKE FILLING

Mix together the chicken, rice, coconut, chili sauce, cilantro, basil, onion, lime juice and zest in a medium non-reactive bowl. Cover and refrigerate until use.

Step 2: PREPARE CUCUMBER CUPS

Using the tines of a dinner fork, scrape down the length of the cucumber to decoratively remove some of the peel. Cut the cucumbers into 1-inch sections. Using a melon baller or small teaspoon, make a little cup by removing a bit of the cucumber flesh, leaving the bottom ¼ inch intact. Chop the removed cucumber flesh and stir into the filling.

Step 3: FILL CUPS AND SERVE

Using a small spoon, generously fill each cucumber cup. Arrange on a serving platter and sprinkle with black sesame seeds.

• MAKES 10-12 SERVINGS •

Hoisin Chicken Summer Rolls

Authentic Asian flavors made right at home!

2	cups shredded rotisserie chicken
1	cup prepared hoisin sauce, divided
1	green onion, sliced thinly on the bias
2	ounces cellophane noodles
2	teaspoons toasted sesame oil
2	cups baby spinach leaves
1	small carrot, grated and divided
8	12-inch round sheets rice paper
¼	cup finely chopped peanuts

Step 1: SEASON CHICKEN

Mix together the chicken, ½ cup of hoisin sauce, and green onion in a small bowl. Set aside.

Step 2: PREPARE CELLOPHANE NOODLES

Place the noodles in a medium bowl. Cover with boiling water. Let rest until the noodles are soft. Rinse, drain, and toss with sesame oil.

Step 3: ASSEMBLE SUMMER ROLLS

Dip a sheet of rice paper in a shallow pan of hot (115° F) water for a few seconds. Remove and place on a damp towel. Arrange several spinach leaves in a row about 2 inches from the edge. Place one eighth of the chicken on top of the spinach and sprinkle with one eighth of the carrot. Fold the summer rolls up, burrito style. Cover with a damp towel while assembling the remaining rolls.

Step 4: GARNISH AND SERVE

Pour the remaining hoisin sauce in a small dipping bowl; place in the center of a large serving platter. Cut the summer rolls in half and arrange on the serving platter. Sprinkle with peanuts and serve.

• MAKES 4-6 SERVINGS •

Mini Chicken Pot Pies

Adorable little chicken pot pies packed with all the comforting flavor of their full-sized cousins.

½	cup diced rotisserie chicken
¼	cup frozen peas and carrots, thawed
¼	cup frozen Southern-style hash brown potatoes, thawed
1	small rib celery, minced
1	green onion, sliced thin
1	12-ounce jar chicken gravy
½	teaspoon fresh thyme leaves
	Approximately 24 round wonton wrappers
	Canola oil for frying
	Kosher salt

Step 1: MAKE FILLING

Mix together the chicken, peas and carrots, potatoes, celery, onion, ½ cup of gravy, and thyme in a small bowl.

Step 2: MAKE POT PIES

Place a heaping tablespoon of filling in the center of a wonton wrapper. Moisten the edges with water. Fold in half, pressing well to seal edges. Place the pie on a parchment-lined baking sheet. Continue to assemble with the remaining ingredients.

Step 3: FRY POT PIES

Pour the oil to a depth of 2 inches in a large Dutch oven over medium high. When oil reaches 350° F, gently place the pies into the oil and fry for about 1 minute on each side, or until crisp and golden. Fry in batches of 6 to 8 pies. Drain on a paper towel-lined plate. Sprinkle with salt and serve while hot. Warm and serve the remaining gravy for dipping, if desired.

COOKS NOTES: To keep the wonton wrappers from drying out, keep them covered with a damp towel as you work.

• MAKES 6-8 SERVINGS •

Ranch Chicken Roundups

Get your party platter done in no time with these tasty morsels.

1	8-ounce package cream cheese, softened
1	teaspoon minced garlic
¼	cup grated red onion
1	4-ounce can diced green chilies, drained
1	green onion, sliced
4	large flour tortillas
2	cups shredded Monterey Jack cheese
4	cups shredded lettuce
2	cups shredded rotisserie chicken
1	2.25-ounce can sliced olives, drained
8	tablespoons cooked bacon pieces
8	tablespoons prepared ranch dressing
2	tablespoons minced parsley

Step 1: MAKE CREAM CHEESE SPREAD

Mix together the cream cheese, garlic, red onion, green chilies, and green onion in a small bowl.

Step 2: ASSEMBLE

Place a tortilla on the work surface and spread evenly with one fourth of the cream cheese spread. Sprinkle with ½ cup of shredded cheese, 1 cup of lettuce, ½ cup of chicken, one fourth of the olives and 2 tablespoons of the bacon pieces. Drizzle with 2 tablespoons of dressing. Roll the tortilla tightly, jelly roll style. Wrap in cellophane paper. Continue assembling, using the remaining ingredients. Refrigerate for 1 hour or up to overnight.

Step 3: GARNISH AND SERVE

Unwrap each roll. Cut into ¾- to 1-inch thick slices. Arrange on a serving platter. Sprinkle with parsley and serve.

COOKS NOTES: For added heat, mix in a couple of teaspoons of diced pickled jalapeños to the cream cheese spread.

• MAKES 8-10 SERVINGS •

Paradise Chicken Cheese Log

Pineapple, chicken and macadamia nuts come together to form a fabulous party appetizer.

2	8-ounce packages cream cheese, softened
1	cup finely diced rotisserie chicken
1	cup canned crushed pineapple, drained
1	teaspoon minced garlic
1	green onion, sliced
1/4	cup grated red onion
1/2	cup loosely packed cilantro, chopped
1/2	teaspoon ground black pepper
1/2	teaspoon ground cayenne pepper
3/4	cup chopped macadamia nuts
1/2	cup toasted shredded coconut (see Cooks Notes, below)
	Various crackers for serving

Step 1: COMBINE CHEESE MIXTURE

Mix together the cream cheese, chicken, pineapple, garlic, green and red onion, cilantro, and black and cayenne peppers in a medium bowl. With wet hands, form the mixture into a log shape.

Step 2: COAT WITH NUTS AND COCONUT

Mix together the nuts and coconut in a pie plate. Roll the cheese log into the nut mixture until completely covered. Wrap the cheese log in plastic and chill for at least 1 hour.

Step 3: ARRANGE AND SERVE

Place the cheese log on a serving platter surrounded by crackers.

COOKS NOTES: Toasted coconut lends a wonderful flavor to this dish and it's simple to make. Spread shredded coconut evenly on an ungreased cookie sheet; bake at 350°F for 10 to 15 minutes, or until golden. Stir periodically to ensure even toasting.

• MAKES 8-10 SERVINGS •

Chicken Taquitos

Muy delicioso!

24	6-inch corn tortillas
1	cup shredded rotisserie chicken
½	cup prepared salsa verde
½	cup frozen Southwest style corn (with onions and bell peppers), thawed
1	cup shredded Mexican cheese blend
¼	fresh cilantro, chopped
	Canola oil, for frying
	Kosher salt to taste
1	cup sour cream (optional)
1	cup salsa verde (optional)
1	cup guacamole (optional)

Step 1: WARM TORTILLAS

Wrap the tortillas in foil and heat in a 350° oven for 15 minutes or until soft and pliable.

Step 2: MIX FILLING

Mix together the chicken, salsa, corn blend, cheese blend, and cilantro in a medium bowl.

Step 3: ASSEMBLE TAQUITOS

Place a heaping tablespoon of filling in the center of a tortilla. Roll into a tube shape, securing with a wooden pick. Continue assembling with the remaining ingredients.

Step 4: FRY TAQUITOS

Pour the oil to a depth of 2 inches in a large Dutch oven and heat over medium high. When the oil reaches 350° F, gently place taquitos into the oil and fry, turning occasionally until golden and crisp. Fry in batches of 6 to 8 taquitos. Drain on a paper towel-lined plate. Sprinkle with salt while hot. Hold in a warm oven while cooking the remaining taquitos.

Step 5: SERVE

Arrange the taquitos on a serving platter with bowls of sour cream, salsa verde, and guacamole, as desired, for dipping.

COOKS NOTES: These can be made ahead of time and frozen. Simply place on a parchment-lined cookie sheet after rolling and freeze for 30 minutes. Remove the picks and package in freezer bags until ready for use. Then, fry as above.

• MAKES 8-10 SERVINGS •

Dolmas

Big Mediterranean flavor in a small package.

20	grape leaves, packed in brine
1	cup Greek yogurt
	Zest from 1 lemon, divided
3	teaspoons minced garlic, divided
4	tablespoons chopped mint leaves, divided
1/4	cup extra virgin olive oil, divided
1/2	cup minced rotisserie chicken
1/2	cup cooked long grain rice
2	green onions sliced
1/4	cup pine nuts, finely chopped
	Kosher salt to taste
1	lemon, sliced (use the one from which the zest was removed)

Step 1: PREPARE GRAPE LEAVES

Bring a large stock pot half full of water to a boil over medium high heat. Drain the grape leaves and place in the boiling water; turn off the heat. Soak for 20 minutes. Drain and rinse the leaves with cold water. Set aside.

Step 2: MAKE DIPPING SAUCE

Mix together the yogurt, all but 1 teaspoon of the lemon zest, 2 teaspoons of garlic, and 2 tablespoons of mint in a small, non-reactive bowl. Cover and refrigerate until use.

Step 3: MAKE FILLING

Mix together half the oil, the chicken, rice, green onions, 1 teaspoon of garlic, 1 table-spoon of mint, 1 teaspoon of lemon zest, pine nuts, and salt in a medium bowl.

Step 4: PREHEAT OVEN

Preheat the oven to 350° F.

Step 5: ASSEMBLE DOLMAS

Place a grape leaf on the work surface, vein side up and stem end toward you. Place 2 teaspoons of the filling in the center of the leaf. Fold stem end over the filling, bring the sides of the leaf toward the center and roll tightly, forming a little cylinder. Continue assembling with the remaining ingredients.

Step 6: COOK DOLMAS

Place the dolmas seam side down in a large shallow baking pan; drizzle with the remaining olive oil. Arrange the lemon slices over the dolmas. Pour in enough water to just cover the dolmas. Cover and bake at 350° F for 20 minutes. Remove dolmas to a serving platter, pat dry with a towel. Cool to room temperature.

Step 7: SERVE

Place bowl of yogurt sauce in the center of serving platter. Arrange the dolmas around the dipping bowl and serve.

• MAKES 6-8 SERVINGS •

Hot Artichoke-Chicken Dip

Be prepared to make a double batch—this one's addictive!

1	8-ounce package cream cheese, softened
1	8-ounce container sour cream
¼	cup mayonnaise
1	cup diced rotisserie chicken
1	14-ounce jar marinated artichoke hearts, drained and chopped
1	4-ounce jar diced pimientos, drained
1	teaspoon minced garlic
2	green onion, sliced, divided
1	cup shredded Havarti cheese
½	cup grated Parmesan cheese, divided
2	tablespoons butter
¼	cup panko (Japanese bread crumbs)

Step 1: PREHEAT OVEN AND PREPARE CASSEROLE DISH

Preheat the oven to 350° F. Spray a 1-quart casserole dish with cooking spray. Set aside.

Step 2: COMBINE

Blend the cream cheese, sour cream, mayonnaise, chicken, artichoke hearts, pimiento, garlic, 1 green onion, Havarti, and ¼ cup of Parmesan in a medium bowl. Spread into the prepared casserole dish.

Step 3: BAKE AND SERVE

Heat the butter on high for 10 to 20 seconds, or until melted, in a small microwave safe bowl. Stir in the panko and remaining Parmesan cheese. Sprinkle evenly over the dip. Bake for 15 to 20 minutes, or until lightly browned. Garnish with green onion and serve with sliced baguettes or crackers.

• MAKES 4-6 SERVINGS •

Monte Cristo Minis

Sweet and savory—a terrific flavor combination!

	Butter, softened
1	baguette, cut into ¼-inch slices (about 32 slices)
2	cups shredded rotisserie chicken
4	Gruyere cheese slices, cut into 6ths to fit onto baguette slices
4	deli ham slices, cut into 6ths to fit onto baguette slices
4	large eggs, beaten
¼	cup whole milk
	Pinch nutmeg
	Pinch kosher salt
	Powdered sugar, for garnish
	Prepared orange marmalade, warmed

Step 1: ASSEMBLE SANDWICHES

Butter one side of each piece of baguette. Place 1 teaspoon shredded chicken on top of 1 baguette slice, followed by a slice of cheese, then ham. Top with a slice of bread, butter side down. Secure with a wooden pick.

Step 2: COOK SANDWICHES

Beat together the eggs, milk, nutmeg, and salt in a medium bowl. Dip each sandwich in egg mixture, covering both sides. Heat a large skillet over medium heat; coat with cooking spray. Place the sandwiches in the skillet; cook for 2 to 3 minutes, or until golden. Remove the wooden picks, turn the sandwiches, and cook for another 2 to 3 minutes, or until golden. Hold the finished sandwiches in a warm oven while cooking the remaining sandwiches.

Step 3: GARNISH AND SERVE

Arrange the sandwiches on a serving platter. Sprinkle with powdered sugar. Place a bowl of warmed marmalade for dipping on the serving platter. Serve warm.

• MAKES 8-10 SERVINGS •

Southern Style BBQ Chicken Mini Corn Muffin Bites

These tasty morsels have a flavor reminiscent of the wonderful pulled pork sandwiches famous in the Southern U.S.

1	6-ounce pakage corn muffin mix
¼	cup chopped cilantro, divided
3	tablespoons mayonnaise
3	tablespoons buttermilk
1	teaspoon granulated sugar
1	teaspoon celery seed
	Kosher salt to taste
	Ground black pepper to taste
½	teaspoon lemon juice
1	cup packaged shredded slaw mix, chopped
1	cup shredded rotisserie chicken
⅓	cup prepared barbecue sauce
2	tablespoons diced red onion

Step 1: MAKE SLAW

In a small bowl, stir together the mayonnaise, buttermilk, granulated sugar, celery seed, salt, and pepper, and lemon juice. Add the slaw mix; stir until well coated. Refrigerate for 1 hour or up to overnight.

Step 2: MAKE MINI CORN MUFFINS

Prepare the muffins according to the package instructions, adding 3 tablespoons of cilantro before mixing. Pour the batter into greased miniature muffin cups. Bake for 10 to 12 minutes, or until a toothpick inserted in a center muffin comes out clean. Cool for 10 minutes in the pan. Remove the muffins to a rack until completely cool.

Step 3: HEAT CHICKEN AND SAUCE

Stir together the chicken and barbecue sauce in a small microwave safe bowl. Heat at 70% power for 1 to 2 minutes, or until heated through. Stir in the red onion and remaining cilantro.

Step 4: ASSEMBLE AND SERVE

Slice each corn muffin horizontally. Place a heaping teaspoon of BBQ chicken on the muffin bottom, followed by a heaping teaspoon of slaw. Cover with the muffin top. Continue with the remaining muffins. Place on a serving platter.

COOKS NOTES: The components of this recipe can be made the day before, then heated and assembled just before serving.

• MAKES 8-10 SERVINGS •

Chicken Florentine Cups
with Lemon-Thyme Mascarpone

Lemon and thyme provide a heavenly backdrop for these addictive little gems.

¼	cup butter
1	large shallot, finely diced
1	clove garlic, minced
4	large eggs, beaten
½	cup milk
	Zest from 1 lemon, divided
3	teaspoon fresh thyme leaves, divided
2	cups herb-seasoned cornbread stuffing mix
1	10-ounce box frozen chopped spinach, thawed and squeezed dry
2	cups diced rotisserie chicken
¼	cup grated Parmesan cheese
1	cup mascarpone cheese, softened

Step 1: PREHEAT OVEN AND PREPARE BAKING PAN

Preheat the oven to 350° F. Spray the cups of 2 miniature muffin pans with cooking spray.

Step 2: MAKE LEMON-THYME MASCARPONE

Stir together the mascarpone, half of the lemon zest, and 1 teaspoon of thyme in a small bowl. Refrigerate until use.

Step 3: COOK ONIONS

Place the butter in a large skillet over medium heat; add the shallot. Cook until translucent. Stir in the garlic; cook 1 minute more. Remove from the heat. Set aside.

Step 4: MOISTEN STUFFING MIX

Mix the eggs, milk, remaining lemon zest, and thyme in a large bowl. Stir in the stuffing mix. Let rest for 15 minutes, or until the liquid is absorbed.

Step 5: COMBINE REMAINING INGREDIENTS

To the bowl of moistened stuffing, add and mix together the shallot-garlic mixture, spinach, chicken, and Parmesan cheese.

Step 6: BAKE

Spoon the mixture in the prepared muffin cups, pressing to compact lightly. Bake in the preheated oven for 15 to 20 minutes, or until lightly browned. Cool in the pan for 5 minutes.

Step 7: GARNISH AND SERVE

Arrange Chicken Florentine Cups on a serving platter. Garnish with a dollop of Lemon-Thyme mascarpone. Serve warm.

• MAKES 10-12 SERVINGS •

Chicken Tostadas with Raspberry-Onion Marmalade

Sweet and savory with just a dash of heat.

8	ounces mascarpone cheese
2	green onions, divided
½	cup chopped loosely packed fresh cilantro leaves, divided
1	tablespoon butter
1	small sweet onion, halved and thinly sliced
1	teaspoon minced garlic
¼	cup balsamic vinegar
	Several drops jalapeño hot sauce, to taste
½	cup prepared seedless raspberry jam
8	tostada shells (flat)
2	cups shredded rotisserie chicken

Step 1: PREHEAT OVEN

Preheat the oven to 400° F.

Step 2: MAKE CHEESE TOPPING

Stir together the mascarpone, green onion, and cilantro in a small bowl. Set aside.

Step 3: MAKE RASPBERRY-ONION MARMALADE

Place the butter in a large skillet over medium heat; add the onion. Cook for 3 to 4 minutes, or until the onion is translucent, stirring occasionally. Add the garlic to the skillet; cook for 1 additional minute. Deglaze the pan with the balsamic vinegar. Stir in the hot sauce and raspberry jam; cook for 3 to 4 minutes, or until the jam is completely melted. Set aside.

Step 4: ASSEMBLE TOSTADAS

Place the tostada shells on a baking sheet. Spread 2 tablespoons of the cheese topping evenly over each tostada shell, followed by ¼ cup of chicken. Drizzle with a heaping tablespoon of the raspberry-onion marmalade. Continue to assemble the remaining tostadas. Bake for 10 to 15 minutes, or until heated through.

Step 5: GARNISH AND SERVE

Place the tostadas on a serving platter. Sprinkle with cilantro and serve.

• MAKES 4-6 SERVINGS •

Tuscan Chicken Bruschetta

Close your eyes as you take a bite and you'll swear you were in the Italian countryside.

1	cup diced rotisserie chicken
8	sun-dried tomatoes, packed in oil, diced
1	6.5-ounce jar marinated artichokes, drained and chopped
1	2.25-ounce can diced olives, drained
¼	cup loosely packed fresh basil leaves, cut into thin strips
1	baguette, cut into ¼-inch thick slices on the bias
¼	cup olive oil
2	garlic cloves
	Kosher salt to taste
	Ground black pepper to taste
	Good quality balsamic vinegar to drizzle

Step 1: COMBINE TOPPING

Mix together the chicken, tomatoes, artichokes, olives and basil in a small, non-reactive bowl. Cover and set aside.

Step 2: PREPARE BRUSCHETTA

Preheat grill to medium high. Brush the bread slices with olive oil and grill about 1 minute per side, or until lightly toasted. Arrange the toasted bread on serving platter.

Step 3: ASSEMBLE AND SERVE

Place a heaping tablespoon of the chicken mixture on the toasted bread. Drizzle with balsamic vinegar and serve.

• MAKES 10-12 SERVINGS •

Mango Chicken Bruschetta

Chili powder adds just the right kick to this unusual appetizer.

½	cup diced rotisserie chicken
½	cup frozen mango chunks, thawed and diced
¼	cup chopped loosely packed cilantro
¼	cup minced red onion
1	teaspoon chili powder
	Kosher salt to taste
	Ground white pepper to taste
1	baguette, cut into ¼-inch thick slices on the bias
¼	cup olive oil
2	garlic cloves
1	green onion, sliced

Step 1: COMBINE TOPPING

Mix together the chicken, mango, cilantro, onion, chili powder, salt, and pepper in a small, non-reactive bowl. Cover and set aside.

Step 2: PREPARE BRUSCHETTA

Preheat a grill to medium high. Brush the bread slices with olive oil and grill about 1 minute per side, or until lightly toasted. Rub garlic on the bread slices. Arrange the toasted bread on serving platter.

Step 3: ASSEMBLE AND SERVE

Place a heaping tablespoon of the chicken mixture on the toasted bread. Sprinkle with green onion and serve.

• MAKES 10-12 SERVINGS •

Fiesta Chicken Layered Dip

Juicy mango is the surprise ingredient in this crowd pleaser!

2	cups shredded rotisserie chicken
1	teaspoon packaged taco seasoning mix
1	15-ounce can black beans, rinsed and drained
1	16-ounce jar salsa verde
2	avocados, diced
	Juice from 1 lime
1	16-ounce container sour cream
2	cups shredded Monterey Jack cheese
1	4-ounce can sliced black olives, drained
2	cups lettuce, shredded
1	mango, diced (may substitute frozen mango, thawed)
4	green onions, sliced
	Tortilla chips

Step 1: SEASON CHICKEN

Stir together the chicken and taco seasoning mix in a small bowl. Set aside.

Step 2: SEASON BEANS

Stir together the beans and salsa verde in a small microwave safe bowl. Loosely cover with plastic wrap; heat on 70% power for 1 to 2 minutes, or until heated through. Cool to room temperature.

Step 3: PREPARE AVOCADO

In a small bowl, toss together the diced avocado and lime juice. Set aside.

Step 4: ASSEMBLE AND SERVE

Pour the black beans mixture in a 9 x 13 inch shallow casserole dish; spread evenly. Layer the chicken, sour cream, cheese, olives, lettuce, mango, avocado, and green onions in that order. Serve with tortilla chips.

COOKS NOTES: Blue corn tortilla chips are especially nice with this fiesta maker!

• MAKES 6-8 SERVINGS •

SOUPS

Bombay Tomato-Chicken Soup

Curry and chutney update classic tomato soup with Indian zest!

2	tablespoons olive oil
1	cup frozen diced onion
1	small Granny Smith apple, peeled, cored, and diced
1	small carrot, diced
1	rib celery, diced
3	teaspoons curry powder
2	tablespoons all-purpose flour
4	cups chicken broth
1	28-ounce can crushed tomatoes
¼	cup mango chutney
2	cups diced rotisserie chicken
	Kosher salt to taste
	Ground black pepper to taste
1	green onion, thinly sliced

Step 1: SWEAT VEGETABLES

Pour the oil in a large stock pot over medium heat; stir in the onion, apple, carrot, and celery. Cook, stirring frequently, for 4 to 6 minutes or until onions are translucent.

Step 2: MAKE SOUP

Sprinkle in the curry powder; cook, stirring constantly, for 1 to 2 minutes or until fragrant. Stir in the flour; cook, stirring constantly, for 2 to 3 minutes or until golden. Add the chicken broth; stir until smooth. Stir in the crushed tomatoes, chutney, and chicken. Reduce the heat to low; simmer for 15 to 20 minutes or until the carrots are tender.

Step 3: GARNISH AND SERVE

Check the seasoning, adding salt and pepper as needed. Ladle into soup bowls and garnish with green onion.

COOKS NOTES: For a fun take on tomato soup and grilled cheese sandwiches, serve this with Naan grilled with shredded white Cheddar.

• MAKES 4-6 SERVINGS •

Classic Chicken Noodle Soup

Slow simmered flavors at the speed of fast food.

1	tablespoon olive oil
1	cup frozen diced onions
1	cup frozen diced carrots
2	ribs celery, diced
1	teaspoon minced garlic
8	cups chicken broth
1	bay leaf
6	peppercorns
3	cups egg noodles
2	cups diced rotisserie chicken
1	teaspoon fresh thyme leaves
	Kosher salt to taste
	Ground black pepper to taste

Step 1: SWEAT VEGETABLES

Pour the oil in a large stock pot over medium heat; add the onions, carrots, and celery. Cook for 3 to 4 minutes or until the onion is translucent. Stir in the garlic and cook 1 minute more.

Step 2: BEGIN SOUP

Stir in the chicken broth, bay leaf, and pepper corns. Bring to a boil; cook for 10 minutes.

Step 3: ADD NOODLES AND CHICKEN

Stir in the egg noodles, chicken, and thyme leaves. Return to a boil and cook for 8 to 10 minutes or until the noodles are just tender. Discard the bay leaf and peppercorns. Check the seasoning, adding salt and pepper as needed.

• MAKES 6-8 SERVINGS •

Chicken and Black Eyed Pea Soup

Southern comfort in each tasty spoonful.

2	tablespoons canola oil
2	slices bacon, diced
1	cup frozen diced onion
1	carrot, diced
2	teaspoons minced garlic
1	teaspoon ground cumin
½	teaspoon cayenne pepper
2	15.5-ounce cans black eyed peas, rinsed and drained
4	cups chicken broth
1	6-ounce can tomato paste
2	cups diced rotisserie chicken
2	cups chopped greens
	Kosher salt to taste
	Ground black pepper to taste
1	teaspoon lemon juice
¼	cup grated Cotija cheese

Step 1: SWEAT VEGETABLES

Pour the oil in a large stock pot over medium heat; stir in the bacon, onion, and carrot. Cook, stirring frequently, until the bacon is crisp and vegetables are soft. Stir in the garlic, cumin, and cayenne pepper.

Step 2: MAKE SOUP

Stir in the black eyed peas, broth, tomato paste, and chicken. Bring to a boil, stirring occasionally. Reduce the heat to low; simmer for 20 minutes.

Step 3: ADD GREENS

Stir in the greens; simmer 10 minutes more. Check the seasoning, adding salt and pepper as needed.

Step 4: FINISH AND SERVE

Stir the lemon juice into the soup. Ladle into serving bowls. Sprinkle with Cojita and serve.

COOKS NOTES: Cojita is a Mexican cheese found in the Latin sections of the dairy case and is similar to Parmesan.

• MAKES 4-6 SERVINGS •

Chicken Enchilada Soup with Polenta Cakes

All the zest of enchiladas found in each scrumptious spoonful.

2	tablespoons olive oil, divided
1	cup frozen diced onion
2	teaspoons minced garlic
1	15-ounce can black beans, rinsed and drained
5	cups chicken broth
1	cup enchilada sauce
2	cups shredded rotisserie chicken
½	cup loosely packed cilantro, chopped
1	teaspoon lime juice
	Kosher salt to taste
	Ground black pepper to taste
6	½-inch thick slices prepared polenta
1	cup shredded Cheddar cheese

Step 1: SWEAT ONIONS

Pour 1 tablespoon of the oil in a large stock pot over medium heat; stir in the onion. Cook, stirring frequently, for 4 to 6 minutes, or until translucent. Stir in the garlic and cook 1 minute more.

Step 2: MAKE SOUP

Stir in the black beans, chicken broth, enchilada sauce and chicken; bring to a boil. Reduce the heat to low; simmer for 15 to 20 minutes.

Step 3: CHECK SEASONING

Stir in the cilantro and lime juice; simmer 5 minute more. Check the seasoning, adding salt and pepper as needed.

Step 4: FRY POLENTA

Drizzle remaining oil in a large skillet over medium high heat. Place polenta slices in skillet; cook for 3 to 4 minutes, turning half way through the cooking time, or until golden.

Step 5: GARNISH AND SERVE

Ladle soup into serving bowls; top with a polenta cake. Sprinkle with cheese and serve.

COOKS NOTES: Prepared polenta is available in chubs similar to breakfast sausage and can be found in the pasta section of most well-stocked markets.

• MAKES 4-6 SERVINGS •

Chicken Tortilla Soup

Full of spice, this soup satisfies your craving for Southwest flavor.

2	tablespoons olive oil
1	cup frozen diced onions
2	cups frozen Southwest style corn (with onions and bell peppers)
1	15-ounce can black beans, rinsed and drained
4	cups chicken broth
1	teaspoon ground cumin
2	cups prepared chunky salsa, medium heat
2	cups diced rotisserie chicken
4	small corn tortillas, halved and sliced into ½-inch strips
½	cup loosely packed cilantro, stems removed
½	cup sour cream

Step 1: SWEAT VEGETABLES

Pour the oil in a large stock pot over medium heat; add the onions and corn mix. Cook for 4 to 6 minutes or until onions are translucent.

Step 2: MAKE SOUP

Add the beans, broth, cumin, salsa, and chicken to the pot; bring to a boil, stirring occasionally.

Step 3: ADD TORTILLAS

Stir in the tortillas and cilantro. Reduce the heat to low and simmer for 10 minutes.

Step 4: GARNISH AND SERVE

Ladle into serving bowls. Top with a dollop of sour cream and serve.

• MAKES 4-6 SERVINGS •

Cream of Chicken and Potato Soup with Cheddar Cheese

Cheesy and creamy, this soup warms you heart and soul.

⅓	cup butter
1	cup frozen diced onion
1	teaspoon minced garlic
¼	cup all-purpose flour
3	cups chicken broth
2	cups frozen Southern style hash brown potatoes
2	cups diced rotisserie chicken
2	cups heavy cream
2	cups shredded Cheddar cheese
	Kosher salt to taste
	Ground black pepper to taste
¼	cup chopped fresh chives

Step 1: SWEAT ONIONS

Place the butter in a large stock pot over medium heat; add the onions. Cook for 3 to 4 minutes or until translucent. Stir in the garlic; cook for 1 minute more.

Step 2: MAKE ROUX

Stir the flour into the stock pot; cook for 2 to 3 minutes or until it starts to turn golden brown. Slowly add the chicken broth, whisking constantly, until thickened and smooth.

Step 3: ADD POTATO AND CHICKEN

Stir in the hash browns and chicken. Bring to a boil, stirring occasionally. Reduce the heat to low and simmer for 10 minutes.

Step 4: FINISH AND SERVE

Stir the heavy cream and Cheddar cheese into the soup. Cook, stirring frequently, until the cheese is melted. Check the seasoning, adding salt and pepper as needed. Ladle into serving bowls. Sprinkle with chives and serve.

• MAKES 4-6 SERVINGS •

Lemongrass Scented Chicken Noodle Soup

Simple and refreshing, this soup is so delicious!

6	cups chicken stock
2	stalks lemongrass, cleaned and coarsely chopped
1	small bunch cilantro
½	cup loosely packed chopped cilantro
1	tablespoon sesame oil
1	large sweet onion (Walla Walla or Vidalia), halved and sliced thin
2	cups diced rotisserie chicken
4	ounces rice noodles
½	cup loosely packed Thai basil, chopped
2	green onions, thinly sliced
2	tablespoons lime juice

Step 1: BEGIN STOCK

Pour the chicken stock into a large stock pot over medium heat; add the lemongrass and small bunch of cilantro, stems and all. Bring to a boil; reduce the heat to medium and simmer for 30 minutes. Strain, discarding the lemongrass and cilantro. Return the stock to the pot over medium heat.

Step 2: SWEAT ONIONS

Place the sesame oil in a medium skill over medium heat; add the sliced onions. Cook for 3 to 4 minutes or until the onions are translucent. Stir the onions into the stock pot.

Step 3: FINISH SOUP

Increase the temperature to medium high; bring to a boil. Add the chicken and rice noodles; cook for 8 to 10 minutes or until the noodles are soft, but firm. Reduce the temperature to low. Stir in the Thai basil, chopped cilantro, green onion, and lime juice. Ladle into serving bowls. Serve hot.

• MAKES 4-6 SERVINGS •

South American Chicken Soup

Yucca and plantain are unexpected and delicious surprises in this piquant soup.

2	tablespoons olive oil
1	cup frozen diced onion
1	large yucca, peeled and diced
2	cups frozen Southwest style corn (with onions and bell peppers)
1	jalapeño pepper, seeded and minced
2	teaspoons minced garlic
1	plantain, sliced
1	teaspoon ground cumin
1	teaspoon ground coriander
6	cups chicken broth
2	cups diced rotisserie chicken
¼	cup loosely packed cilantro, chopped
	Juice from 1 lime
	Kosher salt to taste
	Ground black pepper to taste

Step 1: SWEAT VEGETABLES

Pour the oil in a large stock pot over medium heat. Stir in the onion and yucca. Cook for 6 to 8 minutes, or until the yucca is fork tender. Stir in the corn mix, jalapeño, garlic, plantain, cumin, and coriander. Cook for 3 to 4 minutes.

Step 2: MAKE SOUP

Stir in the chicken broth and chicken. Bring to a boil. Reduce the heat to low; simmer for 15 minutes or until the vegetables are tender.

Step 3: FINISH AND SERVE

Stir in the cilantro and lime juice. Check the seasoning, adding salt and pepper as needed.

• MAKES 6-8 SERVINGS •

Caribbean Chicken Soup

Sweet potatoes, black beans and jalapeño give this soup its island flavor.

2	tablespoons olive oil
1	cup frozen diced onion
2	medium sweet potatoes, peeled and diced
1	large jalapeño pepper, seeded and minced
2	tablespoons minced ginger
2	teaspoons minced garlic
½	teaspoon ground allspice
6	cups chicken broth
3	cups coarsely shredded rotisserie chicken
2	15-ounce cans black beans, rinsed and drained
3	green onions, thinly sliced, divided
1	cup loosely packed cilantro, chopped
2	teaspoons fresh thyme leaves
2	tablespoons lime juice
	Kosher salt to taste
	Ground black pepper to taste

Step 1: SWEAT VEGETABLES

Place the oil in a large stock pot over medium heat. Add the onion, sweet potatoes, and jalapeño; cook, stirring frequently, for 4 to 5 minutes or until the onions are translucent. Stir in the ginger, garlic, and allspice. Cook for an additional 2 to 3 minutes.

Step 2: ADD BROTH AND BEANS

Pour the chicken broth, chicken, and black beans into the pot; bring to a boil, stirring occasionally. Reduce the heat to medium-low and simmer for 15 minutes, or until the potatoes are tender.

Step 3: FINISH SOUP

Mix half of the green onions and all of the cilantro into the soup. Stir in the thyme and lime juice. Check the seasoning, and add salt and pepper as needed.

Step 4: GARNISH AND SERVE

Ladle the soup into bowls; sprinkle with the remaining green onions. Serve hot.

• MAKES 6-8 SERVINGS •

Chicken and Cabbage Soup

This comforting soup is reminiscent of stuffed cabbage rolls.

2	tablespoons butter
1	large sweet onion, halved and sliced
2	tablespoons minced garlic
3	cups packaged shredded cole slaw mix
4	cups chicken broth
1	28-ounce can crushed tomatoes
2	cups diced rotisserie chicken
2	teaspoons paprika
	Several dashes jalapeño Tabasco sauce, to taste
½	cup uncooked white long grain rice
3	tablespoons chopped fresh basil
	Kosher salt to taste
	Ground black pepper to taste

Step 1: PREPARE SOUP AND SIMMER

Place the butter in a large stockpot over medium heat; add the onion. Cook for 3 to 4 minutes or until translucent. Add the garlic and cole slaw mix; cook for an additional 3 to 4 minutes or until the cabbage is softened. Stir in the broth, tomatoes, chicken, paprika, Tabasco, and rice. Cover, reduce the heat to low, and simmer, stirring occasionally, for 30 minutes or until the rice is tender.

Step 2: FINISH SOUP

Stir in the basil. Check the seasoning, adding salt and pepper as needed. Ladle into serving bowls.

• MAKES 6-8 SERVINGS •

Chicken and Roasted Vegetable Soup

Roasting the vegetables brings out their natural sweetness and really adds dimension to this soup.

3	tablespoons olive oil
1	small head cauliflower, cut into florets
2	large carrots, diced
1	large parsnip, diced
1	large onion, diced
2	teaspoons minced garlic
6	cups chicken broth
2	cups diced rotisserie chicken
1	tablespoon fresh thyme leaves
1	pint heavy cream
	Kosher salt to taste
	Ground black pepper to taste

Step 1: PREHEAT OVEN AND PREPARE PAN

Preheat the oven to 400° F. Pour the oil into a large roasting pan.

Step 2: ROAST VEGETABLES

Toss the cauliflower, carrots, parsnip, and onion in the roasting pan; coat the vegetables with the oil. Roast for 25 minutes. Stir in the garlic. Continue to roast for an additional 5 minutes.

Step 3: MAKE SOUP

Transfer the roasted vegetables to a large stockpot over medium high heat. Stir in the chicken broth, chicken, and thyme. Bring to a boil. Reduce the heat to low; simmer for 15 minutes. Stir in the heavy cream. Check the seasoning, adding salt and pepper as needed.

• MAKES 6-8 SERVINGS •

Chicken Vegetable Soup with Udon Noodles

Chicken noodle soup with a decidedly Japanese flair.

2	tablespoon canola oil
1	cup frozen diced onion
1	teaspoon minced garlic
1	teaspoon grated fresh ginger
2	heads baby bok choy, sliced
½	cup shredded carrot
1	rib celery, thinly sliced on the bias
6	cups chicken broth
2	cups diced rotisserie chicken
1	8-ounce can bamboo shoot strips, rinsed and drained
1	10-ounce package dry udon noodles
1	8-ounce package enoki mushrooms, cleaned and trimmed
	Soy sauce, to taste
	Ground white pepper to taste
1	green onion, sliced thinly on the bias

Step 1: SWEAT VEGETABLES

Pour the oil in a large stock pot over medium high heat. Stir in the onion, garlic, ginger, bok choy, carrot, and celery. Cook for 4 to 6 minutes, until the onions are translucent.

Step 2: ADD BROTH AND CHICKEN

Stir in the broth, chicken, and bamboo shoots. Bring to a boil, stirring occasionally.

Step 3: ADD UDON

Stir the udon into the boiling soup. Return to a boil; cook for 8 to 10 minutes or until noodles are tender but firm.

Step 4: SEASON AND SERVE

Reduce the heat to low; Stir in the mushrooms. Check the seasoning, adding soy sauce and pepper as needed. Ladle into serving bowls. Sprinkle with green onions and serve.

• MAKES 4-6 SERVINGS •

Mushroom Thyme Chicken Soup
with Truffle Oil Drizzle

Fresh thyme and rosemary accentuate the earthy mushroom flavor deliciously in this soup.

1	tablespoon olive oil
2	slices bacon, diced
1	cup frozen diced onion
3	teaspoons minced garlic
2	pounds various mushrooms (crimini, shitaki, morels, trumpet, etc.), cut into bite size pieces
1	tablespoon fresh thyme leaves
1	teaspoon finely minced fresh rosemary leaves
½	cup pinot gris or preferred white wine
3	cups chicken broth
3	cups beef broth
3	cups shredded rotisserie chicken
2	tablespoons truffle oil (optional)

Step 1: COOK BACON

Pour the olive oil in a large stock pot over medium heat; stir in the diced bacon. Cook, stirring occasionally, for 4 to 5 minutes or until crisp. Remove the bacon to a plate.

Step 2: SWEAT VEGETABLES

Add the onion to the stockpot and cook for 3 to 4 minutes or until translucent. Add the garlic and mushrooms; cook for 3 to 4 minutes, stirring occasionally, or until the mushrooms are just beginning to become golden. Add the herbs; cook for an additional 2 minutes or until fragrant.

Step 3: DEGLAZE AND ADD BROTH

Stir the wine into the mushrooms, taking care to scrape all the brown bits up from the bottom of the pot. Add the chicken and beef broths, chicken, and bacon. Bring to a boil. Reduce the heat to low; simmer for 10 minutes.

Step 4: FINISH AND SERVE

Ladle the soup into serving bowls. Drizzle with a teaspoon of the truffle oil. Serve hot.

COOKS NOTES: Serve with a loaf of rustic Italian bread and a crisp salad.

• MAKES 6-8 SERVINGS •

Southwest Style Chicken and Corn Chowder

This rich and creamy chowder recipe is one you'll want to keep in your repertoire.

2	tablespoons butter
1	tablespoon olive oil
1	cup frozen diced onion
6	cups frozen Southwest style corn (with onions and bell peppers)
2	teaspoons minced garlic
1	teaspoon ground cumin seed
¼	cup all-purpose flour
5	cups chicken broth
2	Idaho potatoes, peeled and diced
2	cups diced rotisserie chicken
2	cups heavy cream
	Kosher salt to taste
	Ground black pepper to taste
	Jalapeño Tabasco to taste
½	cup loosely packed cilantro, chopped

Step 1: SWEAT VEGETABLES

Heat the butter and olive oil in a soup pot over medium heat. Add the onion, corn, garlic, and cumin. Cook until the onion is soft, about 8 to 10 minutes.

Step 2: ADD FLOUR

Sprinkle flour over the onion and corn; cook, stirring constantly, 4 to 6 minutes, or until flour is golden.

Step 3: ADD BROTH AND POTATOES

Slowly whisk in the broth until smooth. Stir in the potatoes and chicken; bring to a boil. Reduce the heat to low; simmer for 15 to 20 minutes, or until potatoes are tender.

Step 4: CHECK SEASONING

Stir in the cream. Check the seasoning, adding salt, pepper and Tabasco to taste. Simmer 10 minutes more.

Step 5: FINISH AND SERVE

Stir in the cilantro and serve.

• MAKES 6-8 SERVINGS •

Creole Chicken and Shrimp Stew

Big Louisiana flavors right at home.

2	tablespoons olive oil
4	cups frozen southwest style corn (with onions and bell peppers)
1	cup frozen okra, thawed
2	teaspoons minced garlic
1	28-ounce can tomato purée
4	cups chicken stock
2	cups diced rotisserie chicken
½	pound frozen fully cooked medium shrimp, peeled and deveined
	Several dashes hot sauce, to taste
1	bay leaf
2	tablespoons fresh thyme
1	tablespoon lime juice
	Kosher salt to taste
	Ground black pepper to taste

Step 1: SWEAT VEGETABLES

Pour the oil in a large stockpot over medium heat. Add the corn, okra, and garlic; cook for 4 to 5 minutes or until just tender. Add the tomato purée, chicken stock, chicken, shrimp, hot sauce, bay leaf, and thyme. Bring to a boil, stirring occasionally. Reduce the heat to low, and simmer for 15 minutes.

Step 2: FINISH STEW

Remove the bay leaf, and stir in the lime juice. Check the seasoning, adding salt and pepper as needed.

• MAKES 6-8 SERVINGS •

Chicken Amandine Soup

Subtle almond enhances the flavor of this creamy soup.

2	tablespoons canola oil
2	tablespoons butter
1	cup frozen diced onion
1	small carrot, grated
1	rib celery, minced
¼	cup all-purpose flour
4	cups chicken broth
1	bay leaf
¾	cup slivered almonds, toasted, divided
1	pint heavy cream
2	cups coarsely shredded rotisserie chicken
	Kosher salt to taste
	Ground white pepper to taste
1	green onion, sliced

Step 1: SWEAT VEGETABLES

Place the oil and butter in a medium stock pot over medium heat. Add the onion, carrot, and celery; cook, stirring frequently, for 3 to 4 minutes or until vegetables are fragrant and soft.

Step 2: MAKE SOUP BASE

Stir in the flour; cook for 2 to 3 minutes or until golden. Slowly whisk in the chicken broth. Cook, whisking constantly, for 4 to 6 minutes or until smooth and thickened. Add the bay leaf and ½ cup of almonds. Bring to a boil, stirring frequently. Reduce the heat to low. Simmer for 15 minutes. Discard the bay leaf. Purée the soup base with an immersion blender until smooth.

Step 3: FINISH SOUP

Stir the heavy cream and chicken into the soup base. Check the seasoning, adding salt and pepper as needed. Simmer for 15 minutes or until heated through.

Step 4: GARNISH AND SERVE

Ladle soup into bowls, and sprinkle with toasted almonds and onion slices. Serve hot.

• MAKES 4-6 SERVINGS •

Chicken Lo Mein Soup

This quick soup is on the table in less than 20 minutes!

6	cups chicken broth
3	tablespoons soy sauce
1	teaspoon grated ginger
2	cups diced rotisserie chicken
1	16-ounce package frozen lo mein and vegetable mix
2	green onions, sliced
	Toasted sesame oil

Step 1: SEASON BROTH

Pour the chicken broth in a large stock pot over medium high heat. Stir in the soy sauce and ginger. Bring to a boil.

Step 2: ADD CHICKEN AND VEGETABLES

Stir the chicken and lo mein mix into the broth. Bring to a boil; cook for 8 to 10 minutes, or until the vegetables are crisp-tender. Stir in the green onions.

Step 3: FINISH AND SERVE

Ladle into serving bowls. Drizzle with sesame oil and serve.

• MAKES 4-6 SERVINGS •

Chicken and Escarole Soup

Served with a crusty loaf of French bread, this makes a perfect light meal.

2	tablespoons olive oil
2	ounces pancetta, diced
1	cup frozen diced onion
2	teaspoons minced garlic
4	cups chicken broth
1	15-ounce can cannellini beans
2	cups diced rotisserie chicken
½	head escarole, coarsely chopped
1	teaspoon lemon juice
	Kosher salt to taste
	Ground black pepper to taste
¼	cup grated manchego cheese

Step 1: COOK PANCETTA AND ENDIVE

Pour the olive oil and a large stock pot over medium heat; stir in the pancetta. Cook for 3 to 5 minutes, stirring occasionally, or until golden. Stir in the onion; cook for 3 to 4 minutes or until translucent. Add garlic; cook for 1 minute more.

Step 2: MAKE SOUP

Stir in the broth, beans, and chicken. Bring to a boil; reduce the heat to low and simmer for 5 minutes.

Step 3: FINISH AND SERVE

Stir in the escarole and lemon juice. Check the seasoning, adding salt and pepper as needed. Ladle into serving bowls and sprinkle with cheese. Serve hot.

COOKS NOTES: Curly endive is a good substitution for the escarole.

• MAKES 4-6 SERVINGS •

Chicken Minestrone

Surprisingly quick, this soup tastes like it's been simmering all day.

1	tablespoon olive oil
1	cup frozen diced onions
2	teaspoons minced garlic
1	15-ounce can red kidney beans
4	cups chicken broth
1	28-ounce can Italian seasoned diced tomatoes
1	6-ounce can tomato paste
2	teaspoons dried Italian seasoning
2	cups diced rotisserie chicken
1/2	16-ounce package frozen Italian blend vegetables
1	cup uncooked small pasta shells
1/2	cup chopped fresh basil
1/2	cup grated Parmesan cheese

Step 1: SWEAT ONIONS

Pour the oil in a large stock pot over medium heat; add the onions. Cook, stirring occasionally, for 3 to 4 minutes, or until translucent. Stir in the garlic and cook 1 minute longer.

Step 2: SIMMER SOUP

Stir in the kidney beans, chicken broth, tomatoes, tomato paste, Italian seasoning, chicken, and vegetables; bring to a boil. Reduce the heat to low; cover and simmer, stirring occasionally, for 10 minutes. Stir in the pasta shells and basil; simmer for 15 minutes or until the vegetables and pasta are just tender.

Step 3: GARNISH AND SERVE

Ladle the soup into serving bowls. Sprinkle with Parmesan cheese and serve.

• MAKES 6-8 SERVINGS •

Chicken-Andouille Gumbo

Savory broth with just the right amount of spice!

¼	cup vegetable oil
2	links (about ½ pound) andouille sausage, halved and sliced
2	cups frozen bell pepper and onion mix, diced
2	ribs celery, chopped
2	cups frozen sliced okra
2	teaspoons minced garlic
¼	cup all-purpose flour
4	cups chicken broth
1	28-ounce can crushed tomatoes
2	cups coarsely shredded rotisserie chicken
1	bay leaf
2	teaspoons fresh thyme leaves
¼	cup loosely packed fresh basil leaves, chopped
¼	cup loosely packed fresh flat leaf parsley, chopped
	Cayenne pepper to taste
	Ground black pepper to taste
	Filé powder, to taste

Step 1: SWEAT VEGETABLES

Pour the oil in a large stock pot over medium heat; stir in the sausage. Cook, stirring occasionally, for 3 to 4 minutes, or until it begins to brown. Remove the sausage to a plate; reserve. Add the bell pepper and onion mix, celery, and okra. Cook, stirring occasionally, for 4 to 6 minutes or until the onions are translucent. Stir in the garlic and cook for 1 minute more.

Step 2: START ROUX

Sprinkle the flour into the stock pot. Cook, stirring constantly, for 4 to 6 minutes, or until dark brown. Slowly stir in the chicken broth. Cook, whisking constantly, for 5 to 7 minutes or until smooth and thickened.

Step 3: COMPLETE GUMBO

Stir in the tomatoes, chicken, sausage, bay leaf, thyme, basil, and parsley. Reduce the heat to low; simmer for 20 minutes. Remove from the heat; discard the bay leaf. Check the seasoning, adding cayenne, salt, pepper, and filé as needed.

COOKS NOTES: Serve with steamed white rice on the side for an authentic New Orleans meal.

• MAKES 6-8 SERVINGS •

Chicken, Wild Rice, and Mushroom Soup

This soup is hearty without being overfilling.

2	tablespoons olive oil
2	tablespoons butter
¼	cup wild rice
1	cup frozen diced onion
1	small carrot, diced
2	ribs celery, diced
2	teaspoon minced garlic
1	teaspoon fresh rosemary leaves, minced
1	8-ounce package sliced mushrooms
3	tablespoons all-purpose flour
6	cups chicken broth
2	cups diced rotisserie chicken
1	bay leaf
	Kosher salt to taste
	Ground black pepper to taste

Step 1: COOK RICE AND VEGETABLES

Place the oil and butter in a large stock pot over medium heat. Stir in the wild rice; cook for 1 to 2 minutes or until you hear the rice begin to crackle. Stir in the onion, carrot, and celery; cook 3 to 4 minutes, stirring frequently, or until the onion is translucent. Stir in the garlic, rosemary, and mushrooms; cook an additional 2 to 3 minutes.

Step 2: MAKE SOUP

Sprinkle the flour over the vegetables; cook, stirring constantly, for 2 to 3 minutes or until the flour is lightly golden. Pour in the chicken broth. Whisk until smooth and thickened, taking care to scrape up the bits stuck to the bottom of the pot. Stir in the chicken and bay leaf. Cover and reduce the heat to low; simmer for 10 minutes or until the chicken is warmed through. Remove the bay leaf. Check the seasoning, adding salt and pepper as needed.

• MAKES 4-6 SERVINGS •

Green Curry Chicken Soup

Spicy and savory flavors are tempered by coconut milk in this Thai inspired soup.

2	tablespoons canola oil
1	large sweet onion, halved and cut into thin wedges
1	8-ounce package sliced mushrooms
1	teaspoon grated fresh ginger
1	13.3-ounce can unsweetened coconut milk
4	cups chicken broth
1	teaspoon green curry paste, or more, to taste
2	cups shredded rotisserie chicken
½	cup loosely packed Thai basil leaves, cut into thin strips
½	cup loosely packed cilantro leaves, chopped
4	cups baby spinach, coarsely chopped
	Juice of 1 lime
	Kosher or sea salt to taste
	Ground white pepper to taste

Step 1: SWEAT VEGETABLES

Pour the oil in a large stock pot over medium heat; add the onion and cook, stirring frequently, for 4 to 6 minutes or until onion is translucent. Add the mushrooms and ginger. Cook until mushrooms are just softened.

Step 2: MAKE SOUP

Stir in the coconut milk, broth, green curry, and chicken. Bring to a boil; cook, stirring frequently, for 10 minutes. Stir in the basil, cilantro, spinach, and lime juice. Reduce the heat to low and simmer for 10 minutes.

Step 3: FINISH AND SERVE

Check the seasoning, adding salt and pepper as needed. Ladle into bowls and serve.

• MAKES 4-6 SERVINGS •

Pollo Posole

Traditional posole is made with pork; this version made with rotisserie chicken is equally tasty.

2	tablespoons olive oil
2	cups frozen diced onions
3	teaspoons minced garlic
1	14.5-ounce can crushed tomatoes
2	teaspoons ground cumin
1	teaspoon dried oregano
1	teaspoon dried thyme
6	cups chicken broth
3	cups diced rotisserie chicken
1	15-ounce can hominy, rinsed and drained
½	cup loosely packed cilantro, chopped, divided
	Kosher salt to taste
	Ground black pepper to taste
2	teaspoons lime juice
1	cup shredded iceberg lettuce
4	to 6 radishes, sliced
3	green onions, sliced
1	cup grated Monterey Jack cheese

Step 1: START SOUP

Pour the oil into a large stock pot over medium heat. Add the onions; cook, stirring frequently, for 4 to 6 minutes or until translucent. Stir in the garlic; cook 1 minute more. Add the tomatoes, cumin, oregano, thyme, chicken stock, chicken, and hominy. Bring to a boil; reduce the heat to low and simmer for 20 minutes.

Step 2: FINISH SOUP

Stir in half the cilantro. Check the seasoning, adding salt and pepper as needed. Stir in the lime juice.

Step 3: GARNISH AND SERVE

Ladle the soup into serving bowls and garnish as desired with lettuce, remaining cilantro, radish, onion, and cheese.

• MAKES 8-10 SERVINGS •

Sweet Potato, Black Bean and Chicken Soup

Jalapeño is in deliciously spicy contrast to the sweet potato in this unusual soup.

1	tablespoon roasted peanut oil
1	cup frozen diced onion
1	sweet potato, peeled and diced
1	jalapeño pepper, seeds and membrane removed, finely minced
1	teaspoon minced garlic
1	15-ounce can black beans, drained and rinsed
6	cups chicken broth
2	cups diced rotisserie chicken
1	teaspoon fresh thyme
	Kosher salt to taste
	Ground black pepper to taste
1	green onion, sliced

Step 1: SWEAT VEGETABLES

Pour the oil into a large stock pot; stir in the onion. Cook, stirring occasionally, for 3 to 4 minutes or until the onion is translucent. Add the sweet potato and jalapeño; cook for an additional 4 to 5 minutes, or until the potatoes begin to soften.

Step 2: SIMMER

Stir the garlic, beans, broth, chicken, and thyme into the stock pot. Bring to a boil, stirring occasionally. Reduce the heat to the heat low; simmer for 15 minutes. Check the seasoning, adding salt and pepper as needed.

Step 3: GARNISH AND SERVE

Ladle into serving bowls. Sprinkle with green onions and serve.

• MAKES 6-8 SERVINGS •

Chicken and Barley Soup

This simple yet hearty soup makes a terrific supper on a cool evening.

2	tablespoons olive oil
1	cup frozen diced onion
3	ribs celery, diced
2	large carrots, diced
1/4	cup pearl barley
8	cups chicken broth
1	bay leaf
3	cups diced rotisserie chicken
1/4	cup chopped flat leaf parsley
1	teaspoon lemon juice
	Kosher salt to taste
	Ground black pepper to taste

Step 1: SWEAT VEGETABLES

Pour the olive oil in a large stock pot over medium heat; stir in the onion, celery, carrots, and barley. Cook for 4 to 5 minutes, or until the onions are translucent.

Step 2: MAKE SOUP

Stir the chicken stock, bay leaf, and chicken into the vegetables and barley. Bring to a boil. Reduce the heat to medium low and simmer for 45 to 55 minutes, or until the barley is tender.

Step 3: FINISH AND SERVE

Stir in the parsley and lemon juice. Check the seasoning, adding salt and pepper as needed. Ladle into soup bowls.

• MAKES 6-8 SERVINGS •

Chicken and Garbanzo Soup

Peruvian flavors influence this warm and savory soup.

2	tablespoons olive oil
1	cup frozen diced onion
2	teaspoons minced garlic
1	15-ounce can garbanzo beans, rinsed and drained
1	14.5-ounce can diced tomatoes
2	cups diced rotisserie chicken
4	cups chicken broth
1	teaspoon coriander
1	teaspoon ground cumin
1	teaspoon allspice
1	small yellow squash, diced
2	teaspoons lime juice
	Kosher salt to taste
	Ground black pepper to taste
½	cup grated Cotija cheese
2	tablespoons finely chopped fresh cilantro

Step 1: SWEAT ONIONS

Pour the oil in a large stock pot over medium heat; stir in the onions. Cook, stirring frequently, for 4 to 6 minutes or until translucent. Stir in the garlic; cook 1 minute more.

Step 2: MAKE SOUP

Stir in the garbanzos, tomatoes, chicken, broth, coriander, cumin, and allspice. Bring to a boil. Reduce the heat to low; simmer, stirring occasionally, for 15 minutes. Stir in the squash. Simmer for 10 minutes more. Stir in the lime juice. Check the seasoning, adding salt and pepper as needed.

Step 3: GARNISH AND SERVE

Ladle into soup bowls. Sprinkle with Cotija and cilantro and serve.

• MAKES 4-6 SERVINGS •

Chicken Cannellini Chili

Serve this hearty chili with cornbread for a truly comforting meal.

1	tablespoon olive oil
1	cup frozen diced onion
3	teaspoons minced garlic
2	teaspoons ground cumin
1	teaspoon dried oregano
4	cups chicken broth
1	15.5-ounce jar medium heat salsa verde
3	15-ounce cans cannellini beans
3	cups diced rotisserie chicken
½	cup cilantro leaves, chopped
	Kosher salt to taste
	Ground white pepper to taste
1	cup shredded Monterey Jack cheese

Step 1: START CHILI

Pour the oil in a large stockpot over medium heat. Add the onion and cook, stirring frequently, for 3 to 4 minutes or until translucent. Add the garlic, cumin, and oregano; cook 1 minute more.

Step 2: SIMMER

Add the chicken broth, salsa verde, beans, and chicken to the stock pot. Bring to a boil, stirring occasionally. Reduce the heat to low; simmer for 30 minutes.

Step 3: GARNISH AND SERVE

Stir the cilantro into the chili. Check the seasoning, adding salt and pepper as needed. Ladle into serving bowls. Sprinkle with equal amounts of cheese. Serve hot.

• MAKES 8-10 SERVINGS •

Chicken Pot Pie Soup

All the comfort of chicken pot pie right in your soup bowl!

3	tablespoons butter
3	tablespoons canola oil
1	cup frozen diced onions
1/3	cup all-purpose flour
4	cups chicken broth
2	cups diced rotisserie chicken
1	16-ounce package frozen peas and carrots, thawed
2	cups frozen Southern style hash browns, thawed
1	bay leaf
1	teaspoon fresh thyme leaves
2	cups cream
1	green onion, sliced

Step 1: SWEAT ONIONS

Place the butter and oil in a large stock pot over medium heat; stir in the onions. Cook, stirring frequently, for 3 to 4 minutes or until translucent.

Step 2: START SOUP

Stir the flour into the stock pot; cook for 2 to 3 minutes, or until it begins to become golden brown. Slowly pour in the chicken broth, whisking constantly, until thickened and smooth. Stir in the chicken, peas and carrots, hash browns, bay leaf, and thyme. Bring to a boil, stirring occasionally. Reduce the heat to low; simmer for 15 to 20 minutes or until vegetables are tender.

Step 3: FINISH AND SERVE

Stir in the cream and green onion. Cook for 10 minutes or until just warmed through; do not boil. Remove the bay leaf; ladle into serving bowls.

COOKS NOTES: For a fun touch, top bowls of soup with pie crust cut outs. Simply unroll refrigerator pie dough and cut out fun shapes with a cookie cutter; bake according to package instructions.

• MAKES 8-10 SERVINGS •

Hot and Sour Chicken Soup

This rendition of the Chinese classic makes use of ingredients found in the regular grocery store.

3	tablespoons sesame oil
1	large sweet onion, peeled, halved and cut into thin wedges
¾	teaspoon red pepper flakes
2	tablespoons minced garlic
2	cups angel hair shredded cabbage
½	cup shredded carrots
8	ounces shitake mushrooms, sliced
¼	cup rice vinegar
¼	cup low sodium soy sauce
1	tablespoon fish sauce
8	cups chicken broth
2	cups shredded rotisserie chicken
¼	cup corn starch
3	tablespoons cold water
2	eggs, beaten
½	cup lightly packed cilantro leaves, chopped
	Ground white pepper to taste
	Kosher salt to taste
1	tablespoon lime juice

Step 1: SWEAT VEGETABLES

Pour the oil in a large stock pot over medium heat; add the onions. Cook for 3 to 4 minutes, or until translucent. Stir in the red pepper flakes, garlic, cabbage, carrots, and mushrooms. Cook for an additional 4 to 6 minutes or until the mushrooms are just softened.

Step 2: MAKE SOUP

Stir in the vinegar, soy sauce, fish sauce, and chicken broth and chicken. Bring to a boil.

Step 3: THICKEN SOUP

Stir together the corn starch and cold water in a small bowl until smooth. Whisk into the soup. Reduce the heat to low; simmer for 10 minutes.

Step 4: SEASON AND FINISH

In a slow stream, pour the eggs into the soup, stirring constantly. Stir in the cilantro. Check the seasoning, adding salt and pepper, as needed. Stir in the lime juice and serve.

COOKS NOTES: Traditional hot and sour soup calls for tree ear mushrooms, try them in addition to the shitakes if you can find them.

• MAKES 6-8 SERVINGS •

Chicken Red Lentil Soup with Lemon Scented Yogurt

Richly seasoned broth complements the chicken and lentils deliciously in this savory soup.

2	tablespoons olive oil
1	tablespoon butter
1	large sweet onion, grated
1	large carrot, shredded
2	teaspoons minced garlic
1	teaspoon ground cumin
1	teaspoon ground coriander
1	15-ounce can crushed tomatoes
5	cups chicken broth
1	bay leaf
1	cup red lentils, sorted and rinsed
2	cups diced rotisserie chicken
¼	cup chopped fresh flat leaf parsley
¼	cup chopped fresh cilantro
	Kosher salt to taste
	Ground black pepper to taste
½	cup plain yogurt
1	teaspoon lemon zest

Step 1: SWEAT VEGETABLES

Place the olive oil and butter in a large stock pot over medium heat. Stir in the onion and carrot; cook for 3 to 5 minutes or until the onion is translucent.

Step 2: SIMMER

Stir in the garlic, cumin, coriander, tomatoes, broth, bay leaf, and lentils. Reduce the heat to low. Simmer for 30 to 40 minutes, or until the lentils are tender.

Step 3: ADD CHICKEN

Stir in the chicken, parsley, and cilantro. Increase to the heat to medium high heat. Bring the soup to a boil, stirring occasionally. Remove the bay leaf. Check the seasoning, adding salt and pepper as needed.

Step 4: GARNISH AND SERVE

Stir together the yogurt and lemon zest in a small bowl. Ladle the soup into serving bowls. Spoon a small dollop of lemon flavored yogurt onto the soup. Serve hot.

• MAKES 6-8 SERVINGS •

Chicken and Kohlrabi Soup

Fresh and light, this soup soothes your soul.

1	tablespoon olive oil
1	tablespoon butter
2	cups diced kohlrabi
1/2	cup shredded carrot
6	cups chicken broth
2	cups diced rotisserie chicken
1	bunch watercress, trimmed
	Kosher salt to taste
	Ground white pepper to taste
	Zest from 1 lemon

Step 1: SAUTE KOHLRABI

Pour the olive oil into a large stock pot over medium heat; add the butter. Stir in the kohlrabi and cook for 8 to 10 minutes or until fork tender. Add the carrot; cook for an additional 1 to 2 minutes or until tender.

Step 2: MAKE SOUP

Stir in the chicken broth and chicken. Bring to a boil over medium high heat, stirring occasionally. Stir in the watercress. Reduce the heat to low and simmer for 10 minutes. Check the seasoning, adding salt and pepper as needed.

Step 3: GARNISH AND SERVE

Ladle into serving bowls. Sprinkle with lemon zest and serve.

• MAKES 4-6 SERVINGS •

SALADS

Creamy Chicken and Pea Salad

Fresh tarragon really livens up this salad.

2	cups diced rotisserie chicken
2	cups frozen sweet peas, thawed
1	pint grape tomatoes
1	cup diced Cheddar cheese
1	small red onion, finely diced
¼	cup loosely packed fresh tarragon, chopped
1	cup sour cream
	Kosher salt to taste
	Ground white pepper to taste
6	butter lettuce leaves
	Additional tarragon for garnish

Step 1: COMBINE SALAD

Mix together the chicken, peas, tomatoes, cheese, onion, tarragon, sour cream, salt and pepper in a medium bowl.

Step 2: ASSEMBLE AND SERVE

Place a lettuce leaf on a serving plate, top with one sixth of the salad mixture. Continue assembling with remaining ingredients. Garnish with tarragon and serve.

• MAKES 6 SERVINGS •

Avocado-Chicken Salad with Melons and Honey Mustard Dressing

Tangy dressing and sweet melons make this chicken salad something special.

3	tablespoons honey
3	tablespoons prepared Dijon-style mustard
2	tablespoons champagne vinegar (or white wine vinegar)
2	teaspoons lemon zest
1/2	teaspoon garlic powder
1/2	teaspoon ground white pepper
1	tablespoon poppy seeds
2	cups diced rotisserie chicken
1	cup diced cantaloupe
1	cup diced honey dew melon
1	large avocado, diced
1	cup seedless red grapes
8	cups torn butter lettuce
1/2	cup cashews, coarsely chopped

Step 1: MAKE DRESSING

Whisk together the honey, mustard, vinegar, lemon zest, garlic powder, pepper and poppy seeds in a medium, non-reactive bowl.

Step 2: MAKE SALAD

Mix together the chicken, melons, avocado and grapes in the bowl with the salad dressing. Cover and refrigerate for an hour, or until completely chilled.

Step 3: ASSEMBLE AND SERVE

Arrange lettuce on a large serving platter, mound with chicken salad. Sprinkle cashews over the top and serve.

• MAKES 6-8 SERVINGS •

Chicken Fajita Salad

The Tex-Mex favorite transformed into a salad.

2	tablespoons canola oil
1	16-ounce package frozen bell pepper and onion mix, thawed
2	teaspoons minced garlic
1	teaspoon ground cumin
½	cup loosely packed cilantro, chopped
½	cup vegetable juice
2	cups coarsely shredded rotisserie chicken
8	cups blue corn tortilla chips
1	7-ounce package chopped romaine salad mix
1	cup prepared guacamole
½	cup sour cream

Step 1: SWEAT VEGETABLES

Pour the oil in a large skillet over medium heat. Stir in bell pepper and onion mix, garlic, and cumin. Cook, stirring frequently, for 4 to 6 minutes or until onions are translucent.

Step 2: FINISH FAJITAS

Stir in the cilantro, vegetable juice and chicken. Cook, stirring occasionally, until chicken is heated through.

Step 3: ASSEMBLE SALAD

Arrange blue corn tortillas on a large serving platter; mound salad mix in the center. Top with fajitas. Garnish with guacamole and sour cream and serve.

• MAKES 6-8 SERVINGS •

Chicken Tostada Compuesta

Make this Mexican restaurant standby right at home.

1	tablespoon canola oil
1/2	cup frozen diced onion
1	teaspoon minced garlic
1	teaspoon cumin
2	cups diced rotisserie chicken
4	corn tostada shells
1	16-ounce can refried beans, warmed
4	cups shredded iceburg lettuce
1/2	cup loosely packed cilantro
1	large tomato, cored and diced
2	cups shredded Cheddar cheese
1/2	cup prepared guacamole
1/2	cup sour cream
1/4	cup sliced black olives
	Prepared salad dressing (ranch or creamy Italian are great choices), to taste

Step 1: SWEAT ONIONS

Pour the oil in a large skillet over medium heat; add the onion. Cook, stirring frequently, for 4 to 6 minutes or until translucent. Stir in the garlic, cumin, and chicken. Cook, stirring frequently, until the chicken is warmed through. Set aside.

Step 2: ASSEMBLE SALAD

Place a tostada shell onto a serving plate. Spread one fourth of the beans on the bottom of the tostada shell. Sprinkle with one fourth of the lettuce, cilantro, tomato, cheese, and seasoned chicken. Continue assembling with the remaining ingredients.

Step 3: GARNISH AND SERVE

Garnish each tostada with a dollop of guacamole, a dollop of sour cream, and several olive slices. Serve with prepared salad dressing to taste.

• MAKES 4 SERVINGS •

Curried Chicken Salad

Cool and juicy sweet with just the right amount of spice.

2	cups diced rotisserie chicken
1/2	cup green seedless grapes, halved
1/2	cup red seedless grapes, halved
1/2	cup diced red onion
2	ribs celery, diced
2	green onions, sliced
1/4	cup loosely packed flat leaf parsley, chopped
1	cup mayonnaise
3/4	cup mango chutney
1	teaspoon curry powder
	Kosher salt to taste
	Ground black pepper to taste
8	cups spring salad mix
1/4	cup bottled balsamic vinaigrette
1/2	cup chopped toasted pecans

Step 1: MAKE CHICKEN SALAD

Mix together the chicken, grapes, diced onion, celery, green onion, parsley, mayonnaise, chutney, and curry powder. Check the seasoning, adding salt and pepper as needed.

Step 2: DRESS AND ASSEMBLE SALAD

Place 2 cups of spring salad mix on a salad plate, and drizzle with one fourth of the vinaigrette. Top with one fourth of the chicken curry salad. Sprinkle with one fourth of the pecans. Assemble 3 remaining salads and serve.

• MAKES 4 SERVINGS •

Grilled Summer Squash and Chicken Tomato Salad

Have an abundance of squash in your garden? Here's a tasty way to put it to use.

¼	cup plus 2 tablespoon olive oil
2	cups baby summer squash (pan, crookneck, and zucchini, cut into bite-sized pieces
¼	cup champagne or white wine vinegar
1	tablespoon lime juice
¼	cup loosely packed fresh basil, chopped
	Kosher salt to taste
	Ground white pepper to taste
1	pint grape tomatoes
2	cups coarsely shredded rotisserie chicken
8	cups baby salad greens

Step 1: PREHEAT GRILL

Preheat a grill to medium high heat.

Step 2: GRILL SQUASH

Toss 2 tablespoons of olive oil and the squash in a medium bowl. Transfer to a vegetable grill basket. Put the grill basket onto the grill; cook, stirring occasionally, for 3 to 5 minutes or until just crisp-tender.

Step 3: MAKE DRESSING

Whisk together the remaining olive oil, vinegar, lime juice, basil, salt, and pepper.

Step 4: ASSEMBLE SALAD

Toss the grilled squash, tomatoes, chicken, salad greens, and dressing in a medium serving bowl and serve.

• MAKES 4-6 SERVINGS •

Mojo Chicken Salad

This flavorful salad is full of Latin flavors.

½	cup extra virgin olive oil
¼	cup orange juice
	Juice and zest from 1 lime
1	small red onion, halved and thinly sliced
½	small jalapeño, seeded and finely minced
2	teaspoons minced garlic
1	teaspoon oregano, chopped
	Kosher salt to taste
	Ground white pepper to taste
1	7-ounce package butter lettuce salad mix
½	cup loosely packed cilantro, leaves and tender stems, chopped
1	15-ounce can hearts of palm, chilled, drained and chopped
1	11-ounce jar nopalitos strips, rinsed and drained (see Cooks Notes, below)
2	cups coarsely shredded rotisserie chicken
1	seedless orange, peeled and segmented
1	cup crumbled queso fresco

Step 1: MAKE MOJO DRESSING

Whisk together the oil, orange juice, lime juice and zest, red onion, jalapeño, garlic, oregano, salt, and pepper in a small, non-reactive bowl. Cover and refrigerate for 4 to 6 hours.

Step 2: ASSEMBLE SALAD

Toss together the salad mix, cilantro, hearts of palm, nopalitos strips, chicken, and dressing in a large serving bowl. Arrange orange segments on top. Sprinkle with queso fresco and serve.

COOKS NOTES: Nopalitos are pads from the prickly pear cactus. Look for them in the Latin foods aisle.

• MAKES 4-6 SERVINGS •

Thai Chicken Cabbage Salad with Peanut Dressing

Fresh Thai flavors really liven up this salad.

¼	cup natural peanut butter, chunky or creamy style
¼	cup sesame oil
½	cup seasoned rice vinegar
¼	cup sweet Thai chili sauce
	Zest and juice from 1 lime
1	16-ounce package slaw mix, rinsed and drained
½	cup loosely packed cilantro, finely chopped
½	cup loosely Thai basil, finely chopped
1	small English cucumber, halved and sliced
½	red onion, finely diced
2	cups shredded rotisserie chicken
½	cup dry roasted peanuts, coarsely chopped

Step 1: MAKE DRESSING

Whisk together the peanut butter, sesame oil, rice vinegar, Thai sweet chili sauce, and lime zest and juice in a large serving bowl.

Step 2: ASSEMBLE SALAD

Toss together the slaw mix, cilantro, basil, cucumber, red onion, and chicken in the same bowl used to make the dressing. Sprinkle with peanuts and serve.

COOKS NOTES: To make this salad ahead of time, keep the dressing and salad separate until serving time.

• MAKES 6-8 SERVINGS •

BBQ Chicken Salad with Corn Bread Croutons

Barbecue favorites come together in one fabulous salad!

1	8.5-ounce package corn bread mix, prepared as directed on the package
2	tablespoons butter, melted
1	teaspoon garlic powder
1	teaspoon dried basil
4	cups coarsely chopped rotisserie chicken
1/2	cup prepared barbecue sauce
1	10-ounce package shredded iceburg lettuce salad mix
1	16-ounce package slaw mix
1	small red onion, peeled and diced
1	cup frozen corn, thawed
1	cup prepared slaw dressing
1/4	cup poppy seeds
2	cups shredded Cheddar and Monterey Jack cheese blend
1	2.25-ounce can sliced olives, drained

Step 1: PREHEAT OVEN AND PREPARE PAN

Preheat the oven to 350° F. Spray a baking sheet with cooking spray.

Step 2: MAKE CROUTONS

Dice half the prepared cornbread into 1-inch cubes. Reserve the remaining cornbread for another use. Toss the bread cubes, butter, garlic powder, and basil in a medium bowl to coat. Evenly spread the cornbread pieces onto the prepared baking sheet. Bake for 10 to 15 minutes, stirring halfway, or until golden and crunchy. Cool and store in an airtight container until ready to use.

Step 3: PREPARE CHICKEN

Mix together the chicken and barbecue sauce in a small non-reactive bowl. Cover and refrigerate until use.

Step 4: ASSEMBLE SALAD

Toss together the salad mix, slaw mix, red onion, corn, dressing, and poppy seeds in a large serving bowl. Sprinkle the cheese over the top. Mound the barbecue chicken in the middle of the salad. Garnish with sliced olives and cornbread croutons.

• MAKES 4-6 SERVINGS •

❈ ❈ ❈ ❈ ❈

Cobb Salad

Classic Cobb Salad is updated with fresh basil and sweet roasted garlic.

8	cups chopped hearts of romaine lettuce
1/2	cup loosely packed basil leaves, chopped
1	teaspoon minced roasted garlic
2	cups diced rotisserie chicken
1/2	cup cooked bacon pieces
3	Roma tomatoes, diced
1	large avocado, peeled, pitted and diced
1/2	cup crumbled blue cheese
2	large eggs, hard boiled and diced
1/2	cup sliced black olives
1/2	cup sliced green olives
1	cup prepared croutons
	Prepared salad dressing

Step 1: ASSEMBLE SALAD

Toss the romaine, basil and garlic in a large salad bowl. Arrange the remaining ingredients decoratively in rows on top of the romaine. Serve with salad dressing on the side.

• MAKES 4-6 SERVINGS •

Chicken Panzanella

Tuscan bread and tomato salad with chunks of juicy chicken.

3	tablespoons balsamic vinegar
⅓	cup extra-virgin olive oil
2	teaspoons minced garlic
	Kosher salt to taste
	Ground black pepper to taste
½	pound loaf rustic Italian bread, crust removed and cut into ¾-inch cubes
3	to 4 large tomatoes, pared and cut into wedges
1	small red onion, peeled, halved and sliced thinly
1	cup loosely packed basil leaves, torn into bite size pieces
1	cup kalamata olives, pitted and halved
3	cups diced rotisserie chicken

Step 1: MAKE DRESSING

Whisk together the vinegar, oil, garlic, salt, and pepper in a small bowl.

Step 2: ASSEMBLE SALAD

Toss together the bread, tomatoes, onion, basil, olives, chicken, and dressing in a large serving bowl and serve.

• MAKES 6-8 SERVINGS •

Edamame-Chicken Cold Rice Salad

This refreshing salad really comes together in no time.

¼	cup seasoned rice vinegar
¼	cup sesame oil
1	tablespoon low sodium soy sauce
2	tablespoons black sesame seeds
4	cups cold cooked jasmine or basmati rice
2	cups shredded rotisserie chicken
1	8-ounce package sliced mushrooms
1	3- to 4-inch piece of daikon, peeled and thinly sliced
1	cup frozen, shelled edamame (soy beans), thawed
1	11-ounce can mandarin oranges, drained
2	green onions, thinly sliced on the bias
4	cups torn butter lettuce leaves

Step 1: MAKE DRESSING

Whisk together the vinegar, oil, soy sauce, and sesame seeds in a medium serving bowl

Step 2: ASSEMBLE SALAD

Toss together the rice, chicken, mushrooms, daikon, edamame, orange segments, green onions, and butter lettuce in the serving bowl containing the dressing. Serve cold.

• MAKES 6-8 SERVINGS •

Mandarin Chicken Salad

This zesty chicken salad is full of Asian flavors.

1	11-ounce can mandarin oranges, drained, juice reserved
½	cup rice vinegar
1	tablespoon soy sauce
¼	cup sesame oil
1	pinch cayenne pepper
½	teaspoon grated ginger
½	teaspoon minced garlic
6	cups chopped hearts of romaine
2	cups packaged broccoli slaw mix
2	green onions, thinly sliced on the bias
2	cups coarsely shredded rotisserie chicken
1	cup sliced toasted almonds

Step 1: MAKE DRESSING

Whisk together the reserved mandarin orange juice, vinegar, soy sauce, sesame oil, cayenne pepper, ginger, and garlic in a small bowl.

Step 2: ASSEMBLE SALAD

Toss together romaine, slaw mix, onions, chicken, and dressing in a salad bowl.

Step 3: GARNISH AND SERVE

Sprinkle with toasted almonds and serve.

• MAKES 4-6 SERVINGS •

Sesame Chicken Slaw

Packaged slaw mixes and rotisserie chicken are huge time-savers in this recipe.

1	cup mayonnaise
¼	cup toasted sesame oil
¼	cup seasoned rice vinegar
½	teaspoon grated ginger
1	teaspoon minced garlic
4	cups angel hair shredded cabbage
2	cups broccoli slaw mix
2	cups diced rotisserie chicken
3	green onions, thinly sliced on the bias
½	cup loosely packed cilantro, chopped
3	tablespoons black sesame seeds

Step 1: MAKE DRESSING

Mix together the mayonnaise, sesame oil, rice vinegar, ginger, and garlic in a small, non-reactive bowl. Cover and refrigerate for at least 1 hour or up to overnight.

Step 2: MIX SALAD

Mix together the cabbage, broccoli slaw, chicken, green onions, cilantro, and dressing in a medium bowl.

Step 3: ASSEMBLE AND SERVE

Place the slaw on a large serving platter. Sprinkle with sesame seeds and serve.

COOKS NOTES: For added crunch, stir in fried Chinese chow mein noodles just before serving.

• MAKES 4-6 SERVINGS •

Waldorf-Inspired Curry Chicken Salad

Sweet and crunchy, this salad has it all!

1	cup prepared mayonnaise
2	teaspoons curry powder
½	teaspoon ground white pepper
3	cups diced rotisserie chicken
2	ribs celery, diced
1	small red onion, peeled and diced
1	small apple, cored and diced
½	cup Thompson seedless grapes
½	cup golden raisins
½	cup dried cranberries
1	7-ounce bag baby greens
1	cup sliced toasted almonds

Step 1: MIX SALAD

Mix together the mayonnaise, curry powder, pepper, chicken, celery, onion, apple, grapes, raisins, and cranberries in a medium non-reactive bowl. Cover and refrigerate for at least an hour or up to overnight.

Step 2: ASSEMBLE AND SERVE

Place the baby greens on a serving platter; mound chicken salad in the center. Garnish with almonds and serve.

• MAKES 4-6 SERVINGS •

Chayote-Chicken Asparagus Salad with Plum Dressing

Asia meets Latin America in this sweet and sour salad.

¼	cup prepared plum sauce
¼	cup prepared Asian sesame salad dressing
1	pound thin asparagus, trimmed and blanched
2	large chayote, peeled and cut into matchsticks
2	cups coarsely shredded rotisserie chicken
2	green onions, sliced thinly
1	red bell pepper, seeded and cut into thin strips
½	cup loosely packed cilantro, chopped
4	butter lettuce leaves, trimmed
2	tablespoons toasted sesame seeds

Step 1: MAKE DRESSING

Whisk together the plum sauce and salad dressing in a small non-reactive bowl. Set aside.

Step 2: TOSS SALAD

Toss together the asparagus, chayote, chicken, onions, bell pepper, cilantro, and dressing in a medium bowl.

Step 3: ASSEMBLE AND SERVE

Place a lettuce leaf on a serving plate. Mound one fourth of the salad on the center of the lettuce leaf. Sprinkle with one fourth of the sesame seeds. Continue assembling with the remaining ingredients.

• MAKES 4 SERVINGS •

Chicken Salad Niçoise

Rotisserie chicken adds a new twist to a classic French salad.

½	cup prepared Italian salad dressing
1	teaspoon Dijon mustard
1	tablespoon loosely packed fresh tarragon leaves, chopped
1	7-ounce package chopped hearts of romaine salad mix
¼	cup loosely packed fresh flat leaf parsley, chopped
4	to 6 small fingerling potatoes, boiled until fork tender, chilled
1	cup frozen whole green beans, thawed
2	cups coarsely shredded rotisserie chicken
1	cup grape tomatoes
¼	cup black olives
¼	cup green olives
½	small red onion, peeled, halved and thinly sliced
2	hard-boiled eggs, peeled and cut into wedges

Step 1: MAKE DRESSING

Whisk together the salad dressing, mustard and tarragon in a small, non-reactive mixing bowl.

Step 2: ASSEMBLE SALAD

Toss together the romaine lettuce and parsley in a large serving bowl. Arrange potato slices, green beans, chicken, tomatoes, olives, onion and eggs over the lettuce. Drizzle with salad dressing and serve.

COOKS NOTES: Be sure to have all the ingredients chilled before serving for best flavor.

• MAKES 4-6 SERVINGS •

❊   ❊   ❊   ❊   ❊   ❊   ❊   ❊   ❊   ❊   ❊

Cool Chicken Pasta Salad

Broccoli slaw adds a delicious crunch to this pasta salad.

1	8-ounce package penne pasta
½	cups mayonnaise
1	cup prepared Italian salad dressing
2	tablespoons chopped flat leaf parsley
1	teaspoon lemon zest
2	cups diced rotisserie chicken
4	cups packaged shredded broccoli slaw
1	cup grape tomatoes
2	ribs celery, diced
	Kosher salt to taste
	Ground black pepper to taste
½	cup roasted sunflower seeds

Step 1: COOK PASTA

Bring a large pot of lightly salted water to a boil. Add the pasta; cook for 8 to 10 minutes, or until al dente. Drain, and run under cold water to cool. Drain again, and transfer to a large, non-reactive bowl.

Step 2: MAKE SALAD

Stir in the mayonnaise, salad dressing, parsley, lemon zest, chicken, slaw, tomatoes, and celery into the cooled pasta. Cover and refrigerate for at least 1 hour before serving. Check the seasoning, adding salt and pepper to taste.

Step 3: ASSEMBLE SALAD

Place salad in a large serving bowl. Sprinkle with sunflower seeds and serve.

• MAKES 6-8 SERVINGS •

Grapefruit Chicken Salad

The sweet-tart grapefruit is an unusual, albeit delicious, surprise in this chicken salad.

2	grapefruits, halved
2	cups diced rotisserie chicken
½	cup mayonnaise
1	teaspoon minced garlic
¼	cup loosely packed basil, chopped
¼	cup finely diced red onion
	Kosher salt to taste
	Ground white pepper to taste
8	cups torn butter lettuce leaves
½	cup toasted and sliced almonds

Step 1: PREPARE GRAPEFRUIT

Cut a small slice from each non-cut end of the grapefruit halves; this will keep the grapefruit from rolling on the plate. Cut the flesh out of each grapefruit using a citrus knife, or a small paring knife. Cut the grapefruit sections out of the membrane; discard membrane. Cut the grapefruit sections in half and place in a medium non-reactive bowl. Reserve the grapefruit shells.

Step 2: MAKE SALAD FILLING

Mix together the chicken, mayonnaise, garlic, basil and red onion with the grapefruit sections. Check the seasoning, adding salt and pepper as needed.

Step 3: ASSEMBLE SALAD

Place 2 cups of lettuce on a salad plate. Fill a grapefruit shell with one fourth of the chicken salad and place on top of the lettuce bed. Continue assembling with remaining ingredients. Sprinkle with almonds and serve.

• MAKES 4 SERVINGS •

Mediterranean Chicken Salad

Classic Mediterranean ingredients come together to make a delicious and healthy salad.

2	cups diced rotisserie chicken
1	large red bell pepper, seeded and thinly sliced
8	cups romaine salad mix
1	cup kalamata olives, drained and pitted
2	green onions, sliced
½	cup prepared Greek salad dressing
2	tablespoons fresh oregano, chopped
2	cups pita chips
4	ounces feta cheese, crumbled

Step 1: MAKE SALAD

In a large salad bowl toss together the chicken, bell pepper, romaine, olives, onions, salad dressing, oregano, pita chips, and half the feta.

Step 2: GARNISH AND SERVE

Sprinkle the remaining feta on top of salad and serve.

• MAKES 4-6 SERVINGS •

Succotash con Pollo Salad

This makes a unique potluck offering—and so easy to assemble!

¼	cup roasted peanut oil
¼	cup cider vinegar
2	green onions, thinly sliced
2	teaspoons minced garlic
1	small jalapeño pepper, seeded and minced
4	cups frozen corn, thawed
1	cup frozen shelled edamame (soy beans), thawed
1	15-ounce can black beans, rinsed and drained
2	cups diced rotisserie chicken
½	cup loosely packed cilantro, chopped
	Kosher salt to taste
	Ground black pepper to taste
½	cup queso fresco

Step 1: MAKE DRESSING

Whisk together the oil, vinegar, onions, garlic, and jalapeño in a medium non-reactive serving bowl.

Step 2: ASSEMBLE SALAD

Toss together the corn, edamame, black beans, chicken, cilantro, salt, and pepper in the serving bowl with the dressing. Cover and refrigerate for at least 1 hour and up to overnight.

Step 3: GARNISH AND SERVE

Toss the salad to redistribute the dressing. Sprinkle with the queso fresco and serve.

COOKS NOTES: This salad is also delicious served on a bed of chopped butter or romaine lettuce.

• MAKES 4-6 SERVINGS •

Chicken and Bacon Chopped Salad

This salad is perfect for a hot summer evening when you don't want to use the stove.

3	cups diced rotisserie chicken
1	5-ounce bag spring lettuce mix
½	cup cooked bacon pieces
1	cup cherry tomatoes, halved
2	carrots, peeled, halved and thinly sliced
1	yellow, orange or red bell pepper, pared, seeded and diced
1	English cucumber, halved lengthwise and thinly sliced
1	cup dried cranberries
1	cup prepared creamy Italian or ranch style salad dressing
1	cup roasted sunflower seeds

Step 1: ASSEMBLE SALAD

Toss the chicken, lettuce, bacon, tomatoes, carrots, bell pepper, cucumber, cranberries, and salad dressing in a medium salad bowl.

Step 2: GARNISH AND SERVE

Sprinkle sunflower seeds over the salad and serve.

COOKS NOTES: Any salad-worthy vegetables are fair game in this salad.

• MAKES 6-8 SERVINGS •

Chicken Salad with Pear and Gorgonzola Dressing

Sweet pears and cranberries are in delicious contrast to the Gorgonzola cheese dressing.

¼	cup pear juice
3	tablespoons white wine vinegar
3	tablespoons walnut oil
1	teaspoon minced garlic
½	teaspoon finely minced rosemary
2	teaspoons Dijon mustard
½	cup crumbled Gorgonzola cheese
1	12-ounce package spring lettuce mix
1	pear, cored and sliced
½	red onion, thinly sliced
½	English cucumber, halved lengthwise and thinly sliced
2	cups coarsely shredded rotisserie chicken
½	cup dried cranberries

Step 1: MAKE DRESSING

Whisk together the pear juice, vinegar, oil, garlic, rosemary, mustard, and Gorgonzola cheese in a small, non-reactive bowl. Cover and refrigerate until use.

Step 2: ASSEMBLE SALAD

Mound lettuce mix on a serving platter. Arrange the pear, onion, and cucumber over the lettuce. Place the chicken on top and sprinkle with cranberries. Drizzle with dressing and serve.

COOKS NOTES: Apple juice is a delicious substitution for the pear juice.

• MAKES 4 SERVINGS •

Greek Chicken Salad

This salad gets its great flavor from fresh herbs and yogurt...healthy eating has never tasted so good!

1	cup plain yogurt
2	teaspoons minced garlic
	Juice from 1 lemon
1	teaspoon lemon zest
¼	cup olive oil
1	tablespoon chopped fresh flat leaf parsley
2	tablespoons chopped fresh oregano
	Kosher salt to taste
	Ground black pepper to taste
2	cups diced rotisserie chicken
1	pint grape tomatoes
1	small red onion diced
½	cup kalamata olives, pitted and chopped
8	cups chopped romaine lettuce
1	cup pita chips, broken into bite size pieces
½	cup feta cheese

Step 1: MAKE DRESSING

Mix together the yogurt, garlic, lemon juice and zest, olive oil, parsley, oregano, salt, and pepper in a small, non-reactive bowl. Cover and refrigerate for at least 1 hour, or up to overnight.

Step 2: ASSEMBLE SALAD

Toss together the chicken, tomatoes, onion, olives, lettuce, pita chips, and dressing in a large serving bowl. Sprinkle with cheese and serve.

• MAKES 4-6 SERVINGS •

Middle Eastern Lentil Salad with Chicken

Contrasting sweet raisins and savory herbs really punch up the flavor in this salad.

½	cup extra virgin olive oil
	Juice and zest of 1 large lemon
¼	cup loosely packed flat leaf parsley, minced
1	teaspoon fresh thyme leaves, minced
1	teaspoon ground cumin
	Kosher salt to taste
	Ground white pepper to taste
¾	cup dry lentils
2	teaspoons minced garlic
1	bay leaf
1	carrot, peeled and thinly sliced
2	cups diced rotisserie chicken
2	cups cooked basmati rice, cooled
½	cup garlic stuffed olives, halved
1	cup golden raisins
8	cups chopped butter lettuce

Step 1: MAKE DRESSING

Whisk together the olive oil, lemon juice and zest, parsley, thyme, cumin, salt and pepper in a medium non-reactive bowl. Cover and refrigerate for at least an hour.

Step 2: COOK LENTILS

Pick over the lentils and place in a large saucepan. Fill with enough water to cover by 3 inches; place over medium high heat. Bring to a boil, stir in the garlic and bay leaf. Reduce the heat to medium; simmer for 15 minutes. Stir in the carrot; cook for 5 minutes or until the lentils and carrots are firm but tender. Drain and cool to room temperature. Discard the bay leaf.

Step 3: ASSEMBLE SALAD

Mix together the lentils and carrots, chicken, rice, olives, and raisins in a medium bowl. Whisk the dressing and toss into the salad.

Step 4: GARNISH AND SERVE

Place the butter lettuce in a large salad bowl; mound chicken-lentil mixture in the center. Serve cool or at room temperature.

• MAKES 4-6 SERVINGS •

Tex-Mex Chicken Salad

Chock full of chicken, black beans and a jalapeño ranch dressing, this salad's got zest!

¾	cup prepared ranch style dressing
2	teaspoons minced garlic
½	teaspoon ground cumin
¼	cup loosely packed cilantro, finely chopped
2	teaspoons diced canned jalapeño peppers, finely minced
2	cups diced rotisserie chicken
1	15-ounce can black beans, rinsed and drained
2	cups shredded Cheddar cheese
2	cups frozen corn, thawed
2	green onions, finely sliced
1	7-ounce bag romaine lettuce, chopped

Step 1: MAKE DRESSING

Mix together the dressing, garlic, cumin, cilantro and jalapeños in a small non-reactive bowl. Cover and refrigerate for at least an hour or up to overnight.

Step 2: ASSEMBLE SALAD

Toss together the chicken, black beans, cheese, corn, green onions, lettuce, and desired amount of salad dressing in a large salad bowl. Serve cold.

• MAKES 4-6 SERVINGS •

SANDWICHES AND WRAPS

Reuben-Style Chicken Sandwiches with Special Sauce

Just a touch of horseradish gives the special sauce on this sandwich a kick.

1½	cups prepared Thousand Island dressing
1	tablespoon prepared cream style horseradish
3	tablespoons capers, chopped
¼	cup butter, softened, divided
1	small onion, peeled, halved lengthwise and sliced
1	cup packaged angel hair shredded cabbage
½	cup jarred sauerkraut, drained and rinsed
2	cups coarsely shredded rotisserie chicken
4	slices Swiss cheese
8	slices light rye bread
4	garlic dill pickles

Step 1: MAKE SPECIAL SAUCE

Stir together the salad dressing, horseradish, and capers in a small non-reactive bowl, Cover and refrigerate for 1 hour or up to overnight.

Step 2: PREPARE KRAUT TOPPING

Place 1 tablespoon of butter in a large skillet over medium heat; add the onion and cabbage. Cook until just crisp-tender. Stir in the sauerkraut; cook until warmed through. Remove from the heat.

Step 3: ASSEMBLE SANDWICHES

Place a slice of bread on a work surface. Spread evenly with special sauce. Cover with one fourth of the kraut mixture, followed by one fourth of the chicken. Top with a slice of cheese and a slice of bread.

Step 4: GRILL SANDWICHES

Butter the sandwich top, and place butter side down in a large skillet over medium high heat. Cook for 1 to 2 minutes or until golden. Butter the top of the sandwich, and flip with a spatula. Cook for 1 to 2 mintues or until the second side is golden. Continue with the remaining sandwhiches.

Step 5: GARNISH AND SERVE

Cut the sandwiches diagonally in half. Place on serving plates. Garnish with dill pickle and a dollop of special sauce.

• MAKES 4 SERVINGS •

Chicken Mole Torta

Rotisserie chicken and prepared mole will get this Mexican sandwich on your plate in no time.

2	cups diced rotisserie chicken
1/2	cup prepared mole
1	tablespoon finely minced cilantro
4	butter lettuce leaves
4	Bolillo rolls, split
4	tablespoons grated Cotija cheese

Step 1: SEASON CHICKEN

Mix together the chicken, mole, and cilantro in a small microwave-safe bowl. Heat at 70% for 2 to 3 minutes or until the chicken is heated through.

Step 2: ASSEMBLE SANDWICHES

Place a lettuce leaf on a roll bottom, and top with one fourth of the chicken mixture. Sprinkle with 1 tablespoon of the cheese and cover with a roll top. Continue to assemble with the remaining ingredients.

• MAKES 4 SERVINGS •

Buffalo Chicken Sandwiches
with Celery Blue Cheese Salad

Chicken, zesty wing sauce and blue cheese...what could be better?

4	ribs celery, sliced thinly on the bias with leaves
1/4	cup finely diced red onion
1/3	cup prepared blue cheese dressing
2	cups diced rotisserie chicken
1/4	cup prepared buffalo wing sauce
4	French sandwich rolls, split
2	cups shredded iceberg lettuce
1/4	cup crumbled blue cheese

Step 1: MAKE CELERY SALAD

Mix together the celery, onion, and blue cheese dressing in a small non-reactive bowl. Cover and refrigerate until use.

Step 2: PREPARE CHICKEN

Mix together the chicken and buffalo wing sauce in a small microwave-safe dish. Heat at 70% power for 1 to 2 minutes or until heated through.

Step 3: ASSEMBLE AND SERVE

Arrange 1/2 cup of shredded lettuce on the roll bottom; cover with 1/2 cup of sauced chicken. Top with one fourth of the celery salad; sprinkle with blue cheese. Cover with roll the top and serve.

COOKS NOTES: You may want to have an ice cold beverage on hand, buffalo sauce can be zesty!

• MAKES 4 SERVINGS •

Chicken Florentine Sandwiches

An unexpected hint of nutmeg really makes this sandwich.

4	sourdough sandwich rolls, split
4	tablespoons chive and onion flavored cream cheese
2	cups baby spinach, washed and trimmed
4	teaspoons olive oil
	Dash nutmeg
8	slices provolone cheese, halved
2	cups shredded rotisserie chicken
1/2	small red onion, sliced thin

Step 1: TOAST ROLLS

Place the rolls open face, cut side up, on a baking sheet. Broil for 1 to 2 minutes or until golden.

Step 2: ASSEMBLE SANDWICHES

Spread 1 tablespoon of cream cheese on the bottom of each roll. Arrange 1/2 cup of spinach leaves over the roll bottom; drizzle with 1 teaspoon of olive oil. Sprinkle with a pinch of nutmeg. Arrange 2 cheese slice halves over the spinach. Follow with 1/2 cup of chicken and onion slices. Top with the remaining slice of cheese.

Step 3: BROIL

Place the sandwich bottoms back under the broiler for 2 to 3 minutes or until the cheese is melted.

Step 4: FINISH AND SERVE

Place a roll top on each sandwich; cut in half. Place on serving plates.

COOKS NOTES: This sandwich is especially delicious served with a zesty marinated three bean salad.

• MAKES 4 SERVINGS •

Chicken Quesadillas with Cranberry Cream Havarti

Sweet-tart cranberry juice infused with spicy jalapeño is the perfect partner for creamy Havarti in this updated quesadilla.

1	tablespoon olive oil
1	small yellow onion, halved and sliced thin
½	jalapeño pepper, seeded and finely minced
1	teaspoon minced garlic
½	cup cranberry juice
2	cups shredded rotisserie chicken
½	cup cilantro, chopped
1	teaspoon lime juice
4	large flour tortillas
4	ounces cream Havarti
½	cup Crema Mexicana
1	green onion, sliced

Step 1: PREPARE FILLING

Pour the oil in a large skillet over medium heat; add the onion and jalapeño. Cook for 3 to 4 minutes or until the onion is translucent. Add the garlic and cook for 1 more minute. Stir in the cranberry juice, and cook until thick and reduced by about half. Stir in the chicken, cilantro and lime juice. Cook until heated through.

Step 2: ASSEMBLE QUESADILLAS

Heat a large ungreased skillet or griddle over medium heat. Place a tortilla onto tthe skillet and heat for 1 minute, or until lightly browned. Flip, arrange one fourth of the cheese over the tortilla, and spread evenly with one fourth of the chicken mixture. Fold in half. Cook until golden brown and the cheese is melted. Remove and keep warm in the oven. Continue making quesadillas with the remaining ingredients.

Step 3: GARNISH AND SERVE

Cut the quesadillas into wedges, garnish with Crema Mexicana and green onion, and serve.

• MAKES 4 SERVINGS •

Sofrito Chicken Manchego Quesadillas

Savory sofrito seasons the chicken perfectly in this quick meal.

4	large flour tortillas
1	cup Spanish sofrito
2	cups shredded rotisserie chicken
1	cup shredded Mexican manchego cheese
1/2	cup loosely packed cilantro, chopped
1/2	cup Crema Mexicana
1	green onion, sliced

Step 1: ASSEMBLE QUESADILLAS

Heat a large ungreased skillet or griddle over medium heat. Place a tortilla onto skillet and heat for 1 minute, or until lightly browned. Flip over; spread one fourth of the sofrito to within 1 inch of the edge of the tortilla, spread evenly with one fourth of the chicken, one fourth of the cheese and one fourth of the cilantro. Fold in half. Cook until golden brown and the cheese is melted. Remove and keep warm in the oven. Continue making quesadillas with the remaining ingredients.

Step 2: GARNISH AND SERVE

Cut the quesadillas into wedges, garnish with Crema Mexicana and green onion, and serve.

• MAKES 4 SERVINGS •

Teriyaki Chicken Quesadillas

Teriyaki chicken, while unexpected, is a delicious addition to this Mexican classic.

2	cups shredded rotisserie chicken
½	cup loosely packed cilantro, chopped
2	green onions, sliced, divided
½	cup prepared teriyaki sauce
4	large flour tortillas
1	cup bean sprouts
1	cup shredded Monterey Jack cheese

Step 1: SAUCE CHICKEN

Mix together the chicken, cilantro, 1 onion, and teriyaki sauce in a medium bowl.

Step 2: ASSEMBLE QUESADILLAS

Heat a large ungreased skillet or griddle over medium heat. Place a tortilla onto the skillet and heat for 1 minute or until lightly browned. Flip over; spread one fourth of the chicken mixture over half of the tortilla. Sprinkle with one fourth of the bean sprouts and one fourth of the cheese. Fold in half. Cook until golden brown and the cheese is melted. Remove and keep warm in the oven. Continue making quesadillas with the remaining ingredients.

Step 3: GARNISH AND SERVE

Cut the quesadillas into wedges; garnish with the remaining green onion and serve.

• MAKES 4 SERVINGS •

Mojo Chicken Sandwiches

Shredded chicken perfectly seasoned with citrus, cilantro, and just a hint of jalapeño.

2	cups coarsely shredded rotisserie chicken
¼	cup red onion, grated
¼	cup prepared zesty Italian dressing
¼	cup loosely packed cilantro, finely minced
½	fresh jalapeño, seeds and pith removed, finely minced
	Juice and zest of 1 lime
2	tablespoons orange juice
4	Bolillo rolls (may substitute sandwich rolls)
1	clove garlic, peeled
4	butter lettuce leaves

Step 1: MAKE FILLING

Mix together the chicken, onion, dressing, cilantro, jalapeño, lime juice and zest, and orange juice in a small non-reactive bowl. Cover and refrigerate for 1 hour or up to overnight.

Step 2: TOAST ROLLS

Cut a small wedge shape lengthwise out of the top of each roll. Place the rolls and roll tops cut side up on an ungreased baking sheet. Broil for 2 to 3 minutes or until golden brown. While still hot, rub the insides of the rolls with the garlic clove.

Step 3: FILL ROLLS

Place a butter lettuce leaf inside a roll; top with one fourth of the chicken mixture. Place a top on the sandwich. Continue to assemble sandwiches with the remaining ingredients.

• MAKES 4 SERVINGS •

Philly Cheese Chicken Sandwiches

Frozen onions and peppers paired with rotisserie chicken make quick work of this fun take on a delicious American classic.

1	tablespoon olive oil
1	tablespoon butter
2	cups frozen bell pepper and onion vegetable mix
	Kosher salt to taste
	Ground black pepper to taste
2	cups coarsely shredded rotisserie chicken, warmed
4	hoagie rolls, split
8	slices provolone cheese

Step 1: SWEAT PEPPERS AND ONIONS

Place the olive oil and butter in a large skillet over medium heat. Add the pepper and onion mix; cook until the vegetables are just crisp-tender. Season to taste with salt and pepper. Set aside.

Step 2: ASSEMBLE SANDWICHES

Place ½ cup of warm chicken onto a hoagie roll; top with 2 cheese slices. Cover with ½ cup of the pepper and onions; top with the roll top. Continue assembling with the remaining ingredients. Serve hot.

COOKS NOTES: For many die hard Philly fans, Cheese Wiz® is a must. You be the judge: replace the provolone with warmed Cheeze Wiz®.

• MAKES 4 SERVINGS •

Tropical Escape Chicken Salad Rolls

The name says it all!

2	cups diced rotisserie chicken
1/2	red onion, diced
1	small red apple, cored and diced
1/2	cup crushed pineapple, drained
1/4	cup golden raisins
1/4	cup flat leaf parsley, finely chopped
1/4	cup prepared honey mustard dressing
1	pinch cayenne pepper
1	small ripe but firm banana, sliced
1/4	cup chopped macadamia nuts
4	large 1/2-inch thick slices Hawaiian sweet bread

Step 1: MAKE FILLING

Mix together the chicken, onion, apple, pineapple, raisins, parsley, dressing, and cayenne pepper in a medium non-reactive bowl. Cover and refrigerate for 1 hour or up to overnight.

Step 2: FINISH AND ASSEMBLE

Stir the banana and macadamia nuts into the chicken salad. Spread one fourth of the salad onto three fourths of a slice of bread. Roll, jellyroll fashion, towards the plain side of the bread. Secure with a wooden pick. Continue assembling with the remaining ingredients. Place on serving plates and serve.

• MAKES 4 SERVINGS •

Chicken-Mango Wraps

Chicken and juicy mango come together to make a quick and zesty meal.

2	cups diced rotisserie chicken
½	diced English cucumber
1	cup diced mango
1	rib celery, diced
½	small red onion, diced
½	cup chopped loosely packed cilantro
1	teaspoon chili powder
2	tablespoons roasted peanut oil
4	cups baby greens
4	large tortillas
	Store-bought balsamic vinaigrette dressing to taste

Step 1: MAKE CHICKEN SALAD

Mix together the chicken, cucumber, mango, celery, onion, cilantro, chili powder, and peanut oil in a medium bowl.

Step 2: ASSEMBLE AND SERVE

Place 1 cup of baby greens on the center of a tortilla; drizzle with the desired amount of salad dressing. Top with one fourth of the chicken salad. Wrap the tortilla burrito style. Continue to assemble wraps with the remaining ingredients.

• MAKES 4 SERVINGS •

Chicken Salad Sandwiches with Curried Mango

Juicy mango and pungent curry add depth to this chicken salad sandwich.

2	cups diced rotisserie chicken
1	large mango, peeled and diced
1/2	cup golden raisins
2	green onions, sliced thinly
1/4	cup loosely packed cilantro, finely chopped
2/3	cup mayonnaise
1	teaspoon mild curry powder
1	teaspoon fresh lemon juice
	Kosher salt to taste
	Ground black pepper to taste
3/4	cup cashews, coarsely chopped
4	butter lettuce leaves
4	large croissants, cut in half, lengthwise

Step 1: MAKE SANDWICH FILLING

In a medium bowl stir together the chicken, mango, raisins, onion, cilantro, mayonnaise, curry powder, lemon juice, salt, and pepper. Refrigerate for 1 hour or up to overnight.

Step 2: FINISH AND ASSEMBLE

Stir the cashews into the chicken salad mixture. Lay a lettuce leaf on the croissant bottom; top with one fourth of the chicken salad. Cover with a croissant top. Continue to assemble sandwiches with the remaining ingredients.

• MAKES 4 SERVINGS •

Chicken Baba Ghanoush Flatbread Sandwiches

Traditional eggplant salad turned into a delicious sandwich.

2	tablespoons olive oil
1	cup frozen diced onion
2	to 3 Japanese eggplants, peeled and cubed
2	teaspoons minced garlic
1	tablespoon fresh lemon juice, or more to taste
	Kosher salt to taste
	Ground pepper to taste
	Dash Tabasco sauce
2	tablespoons finely chopped flat leaf parsley
4	flatbread rounds (approximately 6 inches diameter)
1/2	cup prepared tahini
2	cups shredded rotisserie chicken, warmed
1/4	cup Greek yogurt

Step 1: PREHEAT OVEN

Preheat the oven to 425° F.

Step 2: ROAST VEGETABLES

Place the olive oil, onion, and eggplant in a roasting pan; stir to coat the vegetables well. Roast in the preheated oven for 20 minutes or until golden.

Step 3: FINISH VEGETABLES

Season the roasted vegetables with minced garlic, lemon juice, salt, pepper, and Tabasco sauce; stir in the parsley.

Step 4: ASSEMBLE SANDWICHES

Spread each flatbread with 1/8 cup of tahini, followed by one fourth of the roasted vegetables, then 1/2 cup of chicken. Drizzle each sandwich with 1 tablespoon of yogurt, fold in half, and serve.

• MAKES 4 SERVINGS •

Plum Chicken Baked Buns

Sweet and sour plum sauce add zing to these stuffed delights.

1	cup prepared plum sauce, divided
2	cups finely diced rotisserie chicken
1	green onion, sliced thin
12	each frozen dinner roll dough balls, thawed
1	egg, beaten
1	tablespoon milk
2	teaspoons sesame seeds

Step 1: PREPARE BAKING SHEET

Spray a baking sheet with cooking spray; set aside.

Step 2: PREPARE FILLING

Stir together half of the plum sauce, the chicken, and green onion in a small bowl.

Step 3: ASSEMBLE BUNS

Knead together 2 rolls and press into a ½-inch thick circle. Place one sixth of the filling onto the center of the dough. Pull the dough around the filling forming a ball; pinch to seal the seam.

Step 4: RISE BUNS

Place the buns seam side down 4 inches apart on the prepared baking sheet. Mix the egg and milk in a small bowl; brush onto the buns. Sprinkle with sesame seeds. Cover with a damp cloth and place in a draft free location. Let rise for 30 minutes.

Step 5: BAKE AND SERVE

Bake the buns in a preheated 350° F oven for 25 to 30 minutes or until golden brown. Serve warm with the remaining plum sauce warmed for dipping.

• MAKES 6 SERVINGS •

Monte Cristo Chicken Sandwiches with Rosemary-Scented Raspberry Sauce

Rotisserie chicken replaces the turkey in this classic bistro sandwich.

½	cup seedless raspberry jam
2	tablespoons water
½	teaspoon finely minced fresh rosemary leaves
¼	cup prepared honey mustard
8	slices sourdough bread
8	slices deli ham
2	cups shredded rotisserie chicken
8	slices provolone cheese
2	large eggs
¼	cup milk
½	teaspoon ground nutmeg
	Pinch of kosher salt
	Powdered sugar for garnish

Step 1: MAKE RASPBERRY SAUCE

Place the jam, water, and rosemary in a small saucepan over medium heat. Cook, stirring occasionally, for 3 to 4 minutes or until the jam is melted. Remove from the heat.

Step 2: ASSEMBLE SANDWICHES

Spread 1 tablespoon of mustard onto a slice of bread; top with 2 slices of ham, followed by ½ cup of chicken, then 2 slices of cheese. Cover with a slice of bread. Continue assembling sandwiches with the remaining ingredients.

Step 3: PREHEAT SKILLET

Spray a large skillet or griddle with cooking spray. Place over medium heat.

Step 4: BATTER AND COOK

Whisk together the eggs, milk, nutmeg, and salt in a shallow dish. Dip each sandwich into egg mixture, turning to coat on both sides. Place the sandwiches on the heated skillet; cook for 2 to 3 minutes or until golden. Flip; cook on the second side for 2 to 3 more minutes, or until golden.

Step 5: GARNISH AND SERVE

Cut sandwich in half; place on serving plate. Sprinkle with powdered sugar and serve with a small dish of raspberry sauce for dipping.

• MAKES 4 SERVINGS •

❊   ❊   ❊

Korean-Style Chicken Wraps

The rich flavor of Korean Barbecue is in delicious contrast to the fresh lettuce "shells".

2	cups coarsely shredded rotisserie chicken
½	cup prepared Korean style barbecue sauce
1	green onion, thinly sliced
4	cups cooked jasmine rice
8	large Boston, Bibb, or butter lettuce leaves, washed, and patted dry
2	tablespoons sesame seeds, toasted

Step 1: SEASON CHICKEN

Stir together the chicken and barbecue sauce in a microwave safe dish. Heat at 70% for 2 to 3 minutes, or until just warmed through. Stir in the green onion. Set aside.

Step 2: ASSEMBLE AND SERVE

Place ½ cup of rice into the center of a lettuce leaf. Top with ¼ cup of chicken. Sprinkle with sesame seeds. Place on serving platter. Continue assembling with the remaining ingredients.

• MAKES 4-6 SERVINGS

Stuffed Bread Loaf

Perfect for a special weekend luncheon or brunch.

2	tablespoons olive oil
1	cup frozen diced onion
2	teaspoons minced garlic
2	cups frozen chopped broccoli, thawed
1	8-ounce package sliced mushrooms
2	cups diced rotisserie chicken
1	teaspoon fresh thyme leaves
1	1-pound loaf frozen bread dough, thawed and allowed to rise until double in size
2	cups shredded Monterey Jack cheese
2	tablespoons butter, melted
¼	cup grated Parmesan cheese

Step 1: **PREHEAT OVEN AND PREPARE BAKING SHEET**

Preheat the oven at 350° F. Spray baking sheet with cooking spray. Set aside.

Step 2: **PREPARE FILLING**

Pour the oil in a large skillet over medium heat. Add the onions; cook, stirring frequently, for 3 to 4 minutes or until onions are translucent. Add the garlic, broccoli, and mushrooms. Cook for an additional 4 to 6 minutes, or until the vegetables are softened. Remove from the heat. Stir in the chicken and thyme.

Step 3: **ASSEMBLE LOAF**

Press the bread dough into a flattened rectangle shape. Spread the filling mixture on the dough. Sprinkle evenly with Monterey Jack cheese. Roll up jelly roll style, along the long side. Pinch the ends closed and place on the prepared baking sheet, seam side down.

Step 5: **BAKE**

Using a sharp knife, slash the loaf crosswise every 2 inches. Brush with melted butter and sprinkle with Parmesan cheese. Bake in the preheated oven for 30 minutes or until golden. Let rest for 10 minutes before cutting into thick slices.

COOKS NOTES: Cutting is easier with a serrated blade.

• MAKES 6-8 SERVINGS •

Jerk Chicken Wraps

Spicy Jerk chicken is cooled a bit with mango in this tasty wrap.

2	cups shredded rotisserie chicken
½	cup loosely packed cilantro, chopped
½	cup prepared Jerk marinade
4	burrito sized tortillas, warmed
4	cups chopped butter lettuce
1	mango, peeled and diced
2	green onions, thinly sliced on the bias

Step 1: MAKE FILLING

Mix together the chicken, cilantro, and marinade in a medium bowl.

Step 2: ASSEMBLE AND SERVE

Place a tortilla on a work surface; arrange 1 cup of lettuce, one fourth of the chicken mixture, one fourth of the mango, and one fourth of the onions down the center. Fold the tortilla wrap style. Continue assembling with the remaining ingredients.

• MAKES 4 SERVINGS •

Chicken Beerocks

While traditional beerocks are made with ground beef, this version is just as delicious.

2	tablespoons butter
1	cup frozen diced onion
2	teaspoons minced garlic
2	cups packaged cole slaw mix
2	cups finely diced rotisserie chicken
	Kosher salt to taste
	Ground black pepper to taste
12	each frozen dinner roll dough balls, thawed
1	egg, beaten
1	tablespoon milk
2	teaspoons dried minced onion (optional)
½	cup prepared honey mustard

Step 1: PREPARE BAKING SHEET

Spray a baking sheet with cooking spray; set aside.

Step 2: PREPARE FILLING

Place the butter in a skillet over medium high heat; add the onion. Cook for 3 to 4 minutes or until the onion is translucent. Add the garlic and cole slaw mix. Cook until the cabbage is limp. Remove from the heat. Stir in the chicken, salt, and pepper.

Step 3: MAKE BEEROCKS

Knead together 2 dinner roll dough balls and press into a circle, ¼-inch thick. Place one sixth of the filling onto the center of the dough. Pull the dough around the filling, forming a ball. Pinch the seam to seal well.

Step 4: RAISE BEEROCKS

Place the beerocks seam side down, 4 inches apart, on a baking sheet. Mix the egg and milk in a small bowl; brush onto the beerocks. Sprinkle with minced onion, if desired. Cover with a damp cloth and place in a draft free location. Let rise for 30 minutes.

Step 5: BAKE AND SERVE

Bake the beerocks in a preheated 350° F oven for 25 to 30 minutes or until golden brown. Serve warm with honey mustard for dipping.

• MAKES 6 SERVINGS •

Greek Chicken Pitas

Fresh oregano, kalamata olives and feta cheese…Greek ingredients at their best!

1	cup shredded rotisserie chicken
2	cups loosely packed torn butter or romaine lettuce leaves
½	cup kalamata olives, pitted and sliced
2	teaspoons fresh oregano leaves, chopped
12	grape tomatoes, halved
4	tablespoons prepared Greek salad dressing
2	pitas, halved
4	teaspoons crumbled feta cheese

Step 1: PREPARE FILLING

Toss the chicken, lettuce, olives, oregano, tomatoes, and salad dressing in a medium bowl.

Step 2: ASSEMBLE SANDWICHES

Gently open pita half and fill with one fourth of the filling; sprinkle with 1 teaspoon of feta cheese. Continue to assemble with the remaining ingredients.

• MAKES 4 SERVINGS •

Red Curry Chicken Turnovers

Not your ordinary turnover, this one's packed with flavorful curry!

1	tablespoon sesame oil
½	small yellow onion, halved and sliced thin
1	head baby bok choy, cleaned and sliced thin
½	cup bean sprouts
½	cup diced rotisserie chicken
½	cup coconut milk
2	teaspoons cornstarch
1	teaspoon red curry paste (or more, for added heat)
1	teaspoon lime juice
¼	cup loosely packed cilantro, chopped
	Kosher salt to taste
	Ground black pepper to taste
1	sheet puff pastry, thawed
1	egg, beaten
2	tablespoons black sesame seeds

Step 1: PREHEAT OVEN

Preheat the oven to 400° F.

Step 2: MAKE FILLING

Pour the oil in a large skillet over medium heat; add onion. Cook, stirring frequently, for 3 to 4 minutes or until onion is translucent. Add bok choy and bean sprouts. Cook for an additional 2 to 3 minutes or until bok choy is just softened. Stir in the chicken. Mix together coconut milk, cornstarch and red curry paste in a small bowl; stir into the chicken mixture until smooth and thickened. Remove from heat. Stir in the lime juice and cilantro. Check the seasoning, adding salt and pepper as needed. Set aside.

Step 3: ASSEMBLE TURNOVERS

On a slightly floured work surface, roll the sheet of puff pastry out into a 12x8-inch rectangle. Cut the pastry in half lengthwise, then into thirds crosswise, forming 6 squares. Divide the filling evenly among the 6 squares, leaving a 1-inch border all around. Brush the border with egg; fold each square into half, forming a triangle and covering the filling. Crimp the edges with a fork to form a seal.

Step 4: FINISH AND BAKE

Place the turnovers 3 inches apart on the prepared baking sheet. Brush the tops with beaten egg and sprinkle with sesame seeds. Bake for 15 to 20 minutes or until golden. Cool on a rack for 10 minutes.

• MAKES 6 SERVINGS •

⌘   ⌘   ⌘   ⌘   ⌘

Moo Shu Chicken Burritos

No need for take out to get great Chinese food flavor.

1	tablespoon sesame oil
1	medium sweet onion, halved and sliced thin
4	cups packaged angel hair shredded cabbage
1/2	teaspoon grated ginger
2	green onions, thinly sliced on the bias
2	cups shredded rotisserie chicken
1	cup bottled hoisin sauce
4	burrito sized tortillas, warmed
1/2	cup loosely packed cilantro, stems removed

Step 1: MAKE FILLING

Pour the oil in a large skillet or wok over medium heat; add the onion. Cook for 3 to 4 minutes or until translucent. Stir in the cabbage, ginger, green onion, chicken, and hoisin sauce. Cook until heated through.

Step 2: ASSEMBLE AND SERVE

Place a tortilla on a work surface, arrange one fourth of the chicken mixture down the center. Sprinkle with one fourth of the cilantro. Roll burrito style. Continue assembling with the the remaining ingredients and serve.

• MAKES 4 SERVINGS •

Thai Chicken Burritos

East meets southwest with this easy to put together burrito.

3	tablespoons toasted sesame oil
3	tablespoons seasoned rice vinegar
1	tablespoon low sodium soy sauce
½	teaspoon grated fresh ginger
1	small jalapeño, seeds and membrane removed, finely minced
2	cups angel hair shredded cabbage
1	cup bean sprouts
2	green onions, sliced thin on the bias
1	carrot, grated
4	large tortillas
½	cup prepared Thai peanut sauce plus additional for dipping
2	cups shredded rotisserie chicken, warm
1	cup loosely packed cilantro, chopped
½	cup chopped dry roasted peanuts

Step 1: PREPARE CABBAGE MIX

Whisk together the sesame oil, rice vinegar, soy sauce, ginger, and jalapeño in a medium bowl. Add the cabbage, bean sprouts, green onion, and carrot; toss until the vegetables are well coated. Set aside.

Step 2: ASSEMBLE BURRITOS

Place a tortilla on a work surface. Spread with one fourth of the peanut sauce. Arrange one fourth of the cabbage mixture evenly over the tortilla; top with ½ cup of chicken, and ¼ cup of cilantro and 2 tablespoons of peanuts. Fold the tortilla burrito-style. Continue assembling with the remaining ingredients. Serve with additional peanut sauce for dipping.

COOKS NOTES: For a fun twist on beans and rice, complete this meal with edamame (soy beans) and jasmine rice.

• MAKES 4 SERVINGS •

Chicken Caprese Open-Faced Sandwiches

Served along side a cold pasta salad, this sandwich makes a perfect lunch or light dinner.

4	thick (½-inch) slices from large sourdough loaf
2	cloves garlic
1	large tomato, sliced
	Kosher salt to taste,
	Ground black pepper to taste
8	large sweet basil leaves, cut into thin strips
4	teaspoons olive oil
4	teaspoons balsamic vinegar
1	cup shredded rotisserie chicken
8	slices fresh mozzarella

Step 1: TOAST AND SEASON BREAD

Toast the bread until lightly browned on both sides. While still warm, rub the garlic clove on one side of the bread. Place the toast on an ungreased baking sheet, garlic side up.

Step 2: ASSEMBLE SANDWICH

Arrange tomato slices to cover each piece of toast; season to taste with salt and pepper. Sprinkle with basil leaves; drizzle with olive oil and balsamic vinegar. Next, arrange one fourth of the chicken over the basil leaves. Top with 2 mozzarella slices, placed side by side. Continue to assemble the remaining sandwiches.

Step 3: BROIL

Place the sandwiches in the oven and broil for 1 to 2 minutes or until the cheese is melted. Place on a platter and serve.

COOKS NOTES: This sandwich is equally delicious served at room temperature, just omit the broiling step.

• MAKES 4 SERVINGS •

Chicken Muffaletta Sandwiches

New Orleans is known for Muffalettas, here's one you can make right at home.

½	cup garlic stuffed olives, chopped
1	4-ounce jar diced pimientos
1	6.5-ounce jar marinated artichoke hearts, chopped, liquid reserved
1	rib celery, diced
2	Roma tomatoes, seeded and diced
2	tablespoons chopped fresh oregano
2	tablespoons chopped flat leaf parsley
4	small ciabatta rolls, split
2	cups diced rotisserie chicken
4	slices provolone cheese
¼	cup prepared honey mustard

Step 1: MAKE OLIVE SALAD

Mix together the olives, pimientos (including the liquid), artichoke hearts, and reserved liquid, celery, tomatoes, oregano, and parsley in a medium non-reactive bowl. Cover and refrigerate at for least 1 hour or up to overnight.

Step 2: ASSEMBLE SANDWICHES

Hollow out a bit of the bread from inside the roll bottom to form a little bowl for the olive salad to rest. Place one fourth of the olive salad on each roll bottom. Arrange ½ cup of chicken over the olive salad, followed by a slice of cheese. Spread the cut side of the roll top with 1 tablespoon of the honey mustard. Cover the sandwich with the roll top. Continue to assemble sandwiches with the remaining ingredients.

Step 3: FINISH SANDWICHES

Wrap each sandwich in plastic. Place on a baking sheet; weigh down with a heavy object such as a cast iron skillet. Refrigerate for 1 hour before serving.

• MAKES 4 SERVINGS •

Grilled Chicken Parmesan Sandwiches

Classic Italian ingredients bring this grilled cheese to all new level!

8	slices Italian bread
2	cups shredded rotisserie chicken
4	tablespoons prepared Italian dressing
8	tomato slices
½	cup fresh basil leaves, cut into strips
4	paper thin slices prosciutto
8	¼-inch thick slices fresh mozzarella cheese
2	tablespoons plus 2 teaspoons butter, softened
½	cup grated Parmesan cheese

Step 1: ASSEMBLE SANDWICHES

Place a slice of bread on work surface. Arrange ½ cup of chicken on the bread; drizzle with 1 tablespoon of salad dressing. Top with 2 tomato slices and 2 tablespoons of basil, followed by 1 slice of prosciutto and 2 mozzarella cheese slices. Cover with a second slice of bread. Spread the top of the sandwich with 1 teaspoon of butter; sprinkle evenly with 1 tablespoon of Parmesan cheese. Press the cheese into the butter so it adheres well. Continue assembling the remaining sandwiches.

Step 2: GRILL SANDWICHES

Heat a large skillet or griddle over medium heat. Place the sandwiches Parmesan side down onto the pan. Spread the sandwich top with 1 teaspoon of butter and sprinkle evenly with 1 tablespoon of Parmesan cheese. Press the cheese into the butter so it adheres well. Cook for 2 to 3 minutes or until the cheese begins to brown. Turn the sandwich over with a spatula; cook an additional 2 to 3 minutes or until the second side is golden. Cut in half and serve.

• MAKES 4 SERVINGS •

Devilish Chicken Sandwiches

Fresh herbs really spice up this deviled chicken sandwich.

2	cups diced rotisserie chicken
½	yellow onion, diced
¾	cup mayonnaise, divided
3	tablespoons capers
2	tablespoons spicy brown mustard
1	clove garlic, crushed
1	teaspoon lemon zest
¼	cup loosely packed flat leaf parsley leaves
¼	cup loosely packed cilantro leaves
1	teaspoon ground coriander
	Kosher salt to taste
	Ground black pepper to taste
4	Kaiser buns, split
4	butter lettuce leaves
1	tomato, sliced

Step 1: MAKE DEVILED CHICKEN

Place the chicken, onion, ½ cup of mayonnaise, capers, mustard, garlic, lemon zest, parsley, cilantro, coriander, salt, and pepper in the bowl of a food processor fitted with a metal blade. Pulse several times until the mixture comes together and resembles tuna salad. Cover and refrigerate for 1 hour or up to overnight.

Step 2: ASSEMBLE SANDWICHES

Spread the remaining mayonnaise evenly on the cut sides of the buns. Place a lettuce leaf and a tomato slice on each roll bottom. Next, spoon on one fourth of the deviled chicken and cover with a roll top. Continue assembling sandwiches with the remaining ingredients.

COOKS NOTES: My favorite accompaniments for this sandwich are a pile of salty potato chips and a tall glass of root beer…heavenly!

• MAKES 4 SERVINGS •

Moroccan-Inspired Chicken Tea Sandwiches

Classic chicken salad updated with a Moroccan flair—perfect for afternoon tea, or anytime.

2	cups diced rotisserie chicken
1	medium quince, peeled, cored and diced
½	cup golden raisins
½	cup dried apricots, diced
2	ribs celery, diced
2	green onions, thinly sliced
¾	cup mayonnaise
1	teaspoon curry powder
1	tablespoon lemon zest
¼	cup loosely packed flat leaf parsley, chopped
¼	cup loosely packed cilantro, chopped
¼	cup slivered almonds
40	baby arugula leaves
10	slices pumpernickel bread, crusts removed and cut into 4 triangles
	Sweet paprika

Step 1: MAKE SALAD

Stir together the chicken, quince, raisins, apricots, celery, onions, mayonnaise, curry powder, lemon zest, parsley, and cilantro in a medium non-reactive bowl. Cover and refrigerate for 2 hours or overnight.

Step 2: FINISH SALAD AND MAKE SANDWICHES

Stir the almonds into the chilled salad. Place an arugula leaf on each bread triangle; top with a heaping tablespoon of chicken salad.

Step 3: GARNISH AND SERVE

Arrange the sandwiches on a serving platter. Sprinkle each with a dash of paprika. Serve.

COOKS NOTES: This salad is equally delicious served on a leaf of Belgian endive in place of bread.

• MAKES 12-14 SERVINGS •

Cubano-Inspired Chicken Sandwiches

This sandwich is reminiscent of the popular Cuban one found in Florida.

¼	cup prepared roasted garlic salad dressing
2	teaspoons lime juice
1	tablespoon finely minced cilantro
2	breasts cut from a rotisserie chicken, sliced thinly
4	French style sandwich rolls, split
½	cup yellow mustard
4	slices deli ham
4	slices Jarlsberg cheese
16	dill pickle slices

Step 1: SEASON CHICKEN

Stir together the salad dressing, lime juice and cilantro in a small bowl. Add the chicken, turning to coat. Cover and refrigerate 1 hour or up to overnight.

Step 2: ASSEMBLE SANDWICHES

Place a roll on work surface, spread cut sides with mustard. Arrange one fourth of the chicken on the bottom of the roll. Place 1 ham slice followed by a slice of cheese, then 4 pickle slices. Continue to assemble with remaining ingredients.

Step 3: GRILL SANDWICHES

Heat a large griddle or skillet on medium; spray with cooking spray. Place sandwiches in skillet; weigh down with a second heavy skillet. Cook for 2 to 3 minutes or until golden. Turn sandwiches over with a spatula, cover again with skillet. Cook for an additional 2 to 3 minutes or until golden and cheese is melted. Cut in half and serve while hot.

• MAKES 4 SERVINGS •

ENTREES

Rosemary Chicken and Chevre Stuffed Portabellas

Hearty portabellas are complemented with pungent herbs and just a hint of sweetness from cranberries to make a fabulous meal.

4	large portabella mushrooms
1	tablespoon canola oil
1	tablespoon butter
1	shallot, finely minced
1	teaspoon minced garlic
1	teaspoon finely minced fresh rosemary
¼	cup white wine
4	ounces chevre (goat cheese)
½	cup finely diced rotisserie chicken
3	tablespoons dried cranberries, minced
1	cup dry seasoned bread crumbs
½	cup milk

Step 1: PREHEAT OVEN AND PREPARE BAKING SHEET

Preheat the oven to 400° F. Spray a baking sheet with cooking spray.

Step 2: PREPARE MUSHROOMS

Clean the mushrooms; using a spoon remove and discard the gills. Remove the stem from mushroom caps; mince the stems.

Step 3: START FILLING

Place the oil and butter in a medium skillet over medium high heat; stir in the shallot, minced mushroom stems, garlic, and rosemary. Cook until the garlic is just golden. Pour in the wine; stir, scraping up all the bits stuck to the bottom of the skillet. Remove from the heat. Stir in the chevre, chicken, cranberries, bread crumbs, and milk; mix until the filling comes together.

Step 4: ASSEMBLE AND BAKE

Spoon one fourth of the filling into each mushroom cap, pressing to gently compact. Place the filled mushrooms cap side down on the prepared baking sheet. Continue assembling with the remaining ingredients. Bake for 10 to 12 minutes or until tender. Serve hot.

COOKS NOTE: To prevent the cranberries from sticking to your knife during mincing, spray both sides of the blade with cooking spray.

• MAKES 2-4 SERVINGS •

❀ ❀ ❀

Pronto Chicken Marsala

So rich and flavorful, just as if you simmered it all day long.

2	tablespoons olive oil
2	tablespoons butter
1	8-ounce package sliced mushrooms
1	teaspoons minced garlic
½	cup Marsala wine
1	12-ounce jar mushroom gravy
2	cups coarsely shredded rotisserie chicken
1	teaspoon fresh oregano, chopped
12	ounces penne, cooked al dente according to package instructions
	Grated Parmesan for garnish

Step 1: COOK MUSHROOMS

Place the oil and butter in a large skillet over medium heat; stir in the mushrooms. Cook, stirring occasionally, for 3 to 4 minutes or until softened. Add the garlic and cook for 1 minute more, stirring constantly. Pour in the wine, stirring to scrape all the brown bits from the bottom of the skillet. Stir in the gravy and chicken; bring to a boil. Reduce the heat to low; simmer for 10 minutes. Remove from the heat.

Step 2: FINISH AND SERVE

Stir in the oregano. Place the pasta on a serving platter, top with the chicken marsala. Garnish with Parmesan and serve.

COOKS NOTES: Serve with a Caesar salad and garlic bread for an authentic Italian meal.

• MAKES 4-6 SERVINGS •

Chicken Parmesan Calzone

Authentic Italian flavors right at home!

1	tablespoon olive oil
2	cups frozen bell pepper and onion mix, thawed
¼	cup flat leaf parsley, chopped
2	cups rotisserie chicken, shredded
3	cups prepared garden style pasta sauce, divided
1	cup shredded mozzarella cheese
½	cup grated Parmesan cheese, divided
12	frozen dinner roll dough pieces, thawed

Step 1: PREHEAT OVEN AND PREPARE SHEET

Preheat the oven to 350° F. Spray a baking sheet with cooking spray; set aside.

Step 2: PREPARE FILLING

Place the olive oil in a skillet over medium heat; add the bell pepper-onion mix. Cook for 3 to 4 minutes, or until the vegetables are just tender. Remove from the heat. Stir in the parsley, chicken, 1 cup of pasta sauce, mozzarella, and ¼ cup of Parmesan cheese; stir.

Step 3: MAKE CALZONES

Knead together 3 dinner roll dough balls and press into a 8- to 9-inch circle. Place the dough on a baking sheet. Place one fourth of the filling onto the center of the dough. Fold the dough in half over the filling, crimping with a fork to seal. Continue assembling with the remaining ingredients.

Step 4: BAKE AND SERVE

Place the calzones in the preheated oven; bake for 20 to 30 minutes or until golden. Serve with the remaining sauce warmed and poured on top. Garnish with the remaining cheese.

• MAKES 4 SERVINGS •

Asiago-Chicken Stuffed Portabellas

Pair these gems with a crisp Caesar salad for a terrific light meal.

4	large portabella mushrooms
1	tablespoon olive oil
1	tablespoon butter
1	large shallot, minced
1	teaspoon minced garlic
3/4	cup milk
3/4	cup seasoned Italian bread crumbs
1/2	cup grated Asiago cheese
1/2	cup finely diced rotisserie chicken
4	sun-dried tomatoes packed in oil, minced
1/2	cup loosely packed basil leaves, minced

Step 1: PREHEAT OVEN AND PREPARE BAKING SHEET

Preheat the oven to 400° F. Spray a baking sheet with cooking spray.

Step 2: PREPARE MUSHROOMS

Clean the mushrooms; using a spoon remove and discard the gills. Remove the stem from the mushroom caps; mince the stems.

Step 3: START FILLING

Place the oil and butter in a medium skillet over medium heat; stir in the shallot, minced mushroom stems, and garlic. Cook until the garlic is just golden. Pour in the milk; stir, scraping up all the bits stuck to the bottom of the skillet. Remove from the heat. Stir in the bread crumbs, Asiago, chicken, tomatoes, and basil; mix until the filling comes together.

Step 4: ASSEMBLE AND BAKE

Spoon one fourth of the filling into each mushroom cap, pressing to gently compact. Place the filled mushroom cap side down on the prepared baking sheet. Continue assembling with the remaining ingredients. Bake in the preheated oven for 10 to 12 minutes or until tender. Serve hot.

• MAKES 2-4 SERVINGS •

Baja Style Chicken Tacos

These zesty tacos are crowd pleasers. Serve with black beans and rice and your "south of the border" meal is complete.

20	corn tortillas
2	tablespoons olive oil
1	cup frozen diced onion
2	teaspoons minced garlic
2	cups coarsely shredded rotisserie chicken
1	teaspoon ground cumin
½	teaspoon cayenne pepper
	Juice and zest from 1 lime
2	cups packaged angel hair shredded cabbage
½	cup loosely packed cilantro leaves, chopped
	Lime wedges
	Prepared salsa verde

Step 1: WARM TORTILLAS

Preheat the oven to 350° F. Wrap the tortillas in aluminum foil and place in the oven until soft and flexible, about 12 minutes. Keep wrapped until ready to use.

Step 2: SWEAT ONIONS

Place the oil in a large skillet over medium heat; stir in the onion. Cook, stirring frequently, for 4 to 6 minutes or until translucent. Stir in the garlic, chicken, cumin, cayenne, lime juice and zest; cook for 3 to 4 minutes, or until the chicken is heated through.

Step 3: ASSEMBLE TACOS

Stack 2 tortillas together; top with one tenth of the chicken mixture. Follow with the cabbage, then the cilantro. Squeeze a little lime juice over the taco. Continue assembling with the remaining ingredients. Serve immediately with salsa verde on the side.

• MAKES 4-6 SERVINGS •

Zesty Southwest Style Chicken Pot Pie

Cilantro and green chilis give this comforting classic a southwestern twist.

1	15-ounce box of 2 refrigerated pie crusts, softened as directed on box
2	cups diced rotisserie chicken
1	12-ounce jar chicken gravy
1	4.5-ounce can diced green chiles
1	teaspoon minced garlic
4	cups frozen southwest style vegetables, thawed, drained
2	tablespoons chopped cilantro

Step 1: PREHEAT OVEN AND PREPARE PIE CRUST

Preheat the oven to 400° F. Make the pie crusts as directed on the box for a two-crust pie using a 9-inch pie pan.

Step 2: COMBINE FILLING

Stir together the chicken, gravy, green chiles, garlic, vegetables, and cilantro in a medium saucepan over medium heat; heat until warm.

Step 3: ASSEMBLE AND BAKE

Pour the filling into the crust-lined pie pan. Top with the second crust; seal and flute the edge. Prick the top crust in several places with a fork. Bake for 30 to 35 minutes or until the crust is golden brown. Let stand for 5 minutes before serving. Cut into wedges.

COOKS NOTE: If you like your food with a little more kick, add several drops of hot sauce to the filling before pouring into the crust.

• MAKES 6-8 SERVINGS •

Chicken Carbonara

Served with rustic bread, this is perfect for a quick dinner...or breakfast!

	Kosher salt to taste
12	ounces fettuccine
2	tablespoons olive oil
2	tablespoons butter
4	ounces pancetta, diced
1	cup frozen diced onion
1	teaspoons minced garlic
2	cups diced rotisserie chicken, warm
4	eggs
½	cup heavy cream
	Ground white pepper to taste
¼	cup loosely packed basil leaves, chopped
½	cup grated Parmesan cheese

Step 1: COOK PASTA

Bring a large stock pot of water to a boil; season with salt. Stir in the pasta. Cook for 10–12 minutes or until al dente. Drain, reserving ½ cup of the cooking liquid.

Step 2: COOK PANCETTA

Place the olive oil and butter in a large saucepan over medium heat. Stir in the pancetta. Cook, stirring frequently, for 4 to 6 minutes or until golden. Stir in the onion. Cook, stirring frequently, for 3 to 4 minutes or until translucent. Add the garlic; cook, stirring frequently, for 1 minute more.

Step 3: SAUCE THE PASTA

Toss the cooked fettuccine into the pancetta mixture. Stir in the chicken. In a small bowl, beat together the eggs and cream. Pour into the pasta; toss. Continue tossing until the eggs are soft set. Add cooking water as needed to reach the desired thickness. Check the seasoning, adding salt and pepper as needed.

Step 4: GARNISH AND SERVE

Toss the basil into the pasta; place on a serving platter. Sprinkle with Parmesan and serve.

• MAKES 4-6 SERVINGS •

⌘ ⌘ ⌘ ⌘ ⌘ ⌘ ⌘ ⌘ ⌘

Chicken Pesto Pizza

Much better than delivery, this pizza is over the top.

1	about 1-pound prepared pizza crust dough
1	cup prepared pesto
8	ounces fresh mozzarella, sliced thin
2	cups diced rotisserie chicken
8	to 10 sun-dried tomatoes, cut into strips
1	3.8-ounce can sliced olives
1	green onion, sliced
½	cup pine nuts
½	cup Parmesan cheese

Step 1: PREHEAT OVEN AND PREPARE PAN

Preheat the oven to 400° F. Lightly grease a 12- to 14-inch pizza pan or baking sheet with cooking spray.

Step 2: ASSEMBLE PIZZA

Press the pizza crust dough onto the prepared pan. Spread the pesto to within 1 inch of the pizza edge. Top the pizza with mozzarella, chicken, tomatoes, olives, green onion, pine nuts, and Parmesan cheese.

Step 4: BAKE AND SERVE

Bake the pizza in the preheated oven for 12 to 15 minutes, or until the cheese is melted and lightly golden. Rest for 10 minutes. Cut into wedges and serve.

• MAKES 4-6 SERVINGS •

Chicken Fettuccine Primavera

Creamy sauce packed with Parmesan, garlic and fresh basil—Mangia!

1	tablespoon olive oil
1	tablespoon butter
1	cup frozen diced onions
2	teaspoons minced garlic
1	12-ounce package frozen Italian blend vegetables
2	tablespoons flour
2	cups heavy cream
½	cup chicken broth
2	cups grated Parmesan cheese, divided
2	cups coarsely shredded rotisserie chicken
½	cup plus ¼ cup loosely packed basil leaves, chopped, divided
	Kosher salt to taste
	Ground black pepper to taste
12	ounces fettuccine

Step 1: SWEAT VEGETABLES

Place the oil and butter in a large saucepan over medium heat. Stir in the onions; cook for 3 to 4 minutes or until translucent. Add the garlic and vegetables; cook, stirring occasionally, for 4 to 5 minutes, or until the vegetables are crisp-tender.

Step 2: MAKE SAUCE

Stir in the flour. Cook, stirring constantly, until golden. Slowly stir in the cream, broth, and half of the Parmesan cheese until smooth. Stir in the chicken. Reduce the heat to low; simmer, stirring occasionally for 15 minutes or until thickened. Stir in ½ cup of basil. Check the seasoning, adding salt and pepper to taste.

Step 3: COOK PASTA

Bring a large stock pot of water to boil; season with salt. Cook the pasta in water for 8 to 10 minutes or until al dente. Drain.

Step 4: ASSEMBLE AND SERVE

Pile the drained pasta on a shallow serving bowl. Pour the sauce over the pasta. Sprinkle with the remaining cheese, then basil. Serve hot.

• MAKES 6-8 SERVINGS •

✻　　✻　　✻

Chicken Fettuccine with Walnuts, Cranberries, and Arugula

Sweet cranberries and peppery arugula turn ordinary pasta into something special.

3	tablespoons olive oil
4	ounces pancetta, diced
2	teaspoons minced garlic
½	cup chopped walnuts
2	cups coarsely shredded rotisserie chicken
½	cup dried cranberries
4	cups torn arugula
16	ounces fettuccine, cooked per package instructions, al dente
½	cup grated Parmesan cheese

Step 1: COOK PANCETTA

Pour the olive oil in a large skillet over medium heat; stir in the pancetta. Cook for 2 to 3 minutes or until crispy. Stir in the garlic, walnuts, chicken, and cranberries. Cook until heated through. Toss in the arugula.

Step 2: ASSEMBLE AND SERVE

Place the cooked fettuccine on a large serving platter. Mound the chicken mixture in the center of the pasta. Garnish with Parmesan and serve.

• MAKES 4-6 SERVINGS •

Asparagus Chicken a la Crème

Creamy and decadent, this chicken has a French accent.

2	tablespoons butter
2	cups coarsely shredded rotisserie chicken
1	pint heavy cream
2	teaspoons fresh thyme leaves
½	teaspoon ground nutmeg
	Kosher salt to taste
	Ground white pepper to taste
1	teaspoon baking soda
1½	pounds asparagus spears, washed and trimmed
	Additional thyme for garnish

Step 1: MAKE CHICKEN A LA CRÈME

Melt the butter in a large skillet over medium heat. Add the chicken to the skillet; heat until warmed through. Reduce the heat to low. Pour the heavy cream into the skillet, and simmer gently for 5 minutes, stirring frequently, until the sauce has thickened. Season with thyme, nutmeg, salt, and pepper. Keep warm over low until ready to serve.

Step 2: COOK ASPARAGUS

Bring 2 inches of water to a boil in a large skillet. Season with ½ teaspoon of kosher salt. Add the baking soda to the water. Carefully add the asparagus; cook until the water returns to a boil. Remove immediately, drain, and arrange on a serving platter.

Step 3: GARNISH AND SERVE

Pour the Chicken a la Crème over the asparagus. Sprinkle with thyme and serve hot.

COOKS NOTE: This is especially delicious served with a loaf of French bread.

• MAKES 2-4 SERVING

Chicken Goulash

This goulash is hearty and filling—just like when Mom made it.

2	tablespoons canola oil
1	cup frozen diced onion
2	ribs celery, diced
2	teaspoons minced garlic
2	cups diced rotisserie chicken
1	15.25-ounce can kidney beans, drained
1	28-ounce can crushed tomatoes with basil
1	tablespoon sugar
1	tablespoon paprika
1	tablespoon minced fresh oregano leaves
2	cups chicken broth
2	cups uncooked elbow macaroni
	Cayenne pepper to taste
	Kosher salt to taste
	Ground black pepper to taste
1	cup shredded Cheddar cheese
1	green onion, sliced

Step 1: SWEAT VEGETABLES

Pour the oil in a large saucepan over medium heat; stir in the onions and celery. Cook, stirring occasionally, for 4 to 6 minutes or until the onions are translucent.

Step 2: FINISH GOULASH

Stir in the garlic, chicken, kidney beans, crushed tomatoes, sugar, paprika, oregano, broth, macaroni, and cayenne. Reduce the heat to low; simmer, stirring occasionally, for 20 minutes or until the macaroni is just tender. Check the seasoning, adding salt and pepper as needed.

Step 3: GARNISH AND SERVE

Ladle the goulash into serving bowls. Sprinkle with cheese and onions; serve hot.

• MAKES 6-8 SERVINGS •

Chicken Stuffed Sweet Potatoes

Curry and ginger spice up this unusual meal.

4	large sweet potatoes
2	teaspoons minced garlic
1	teaspoon grated ginger
1/2	teaspoon curry powder
1/4	cup loosely packed cilantro, chopped
1	green onion, thinly sliced
1/2	cup heavy cream
1	tablespoon butter
1	cup diced rotisserie chicken
	Kosher salt to taste
	Ground black pepper to taste

Step 1: PREHEAT OVEN AND PREPARE PAN

Preheat the oven to 400° F. Spray a baking sheet with cooking spray; set aside.

Step 2: BAKE SWEET POTATOES

Prick the washed sweet potatoes several times with a fork. Place on the prepared baking sheet; bake for 30 minutes or until soft.

Step 3: SCOOP OUT POTATOES

Cut a lengthwise slice from the top of each potato, scoop out the flesh from the removed slice and the discard skin. Scoop out the flesh from each potato, leaving a 1/4-inch shell, and place the flesh in a medium bowl.

Step 4: MAKE FILLING

Whip the garlic, ginger, curry powder, cilantro, onion, cream, and butter with the potato flesh. Stir in the chicken. Check the seasoning, adding salt and pepper as needed.

Step 5: FILL AND BAKE

Spoon the filling into the sweet potato shells. Place filled sweet potatoes onto the baking sheet. Return to oven for 15 minutes, or until heated through.

COOKS NOTES: Serve the sweet potatoes on a bed of lightly dressed spring greens for a complete meal.

• MAKES 4 SERVINGS •

Chicken-Boursin Stuffed Pasta Shells

Boursin is a rich and creamy fresh cheese and makes a terrific addition to this dish.

1	cup diced rotisserie chicken
1	9-ounce package frozen creamed spinach, thawed
6	sun-dried tomatoes, packed in oil, minced
1	green onion, sliced
1	5-ounce package garlic and herb Boursin cheese, softened
1	egg, beaten
20	large pasta shells
1	15-ounce jar alfredo sauce
2	cups shredded mozzarella cheese

Step 1: PREHEAT OVEN AND PREPARE CASSEROLE

Preheat the oven to 350° F. Spray a shallow 2-quart casserole dish with cooking spray. Set aside.

Step 2: MAKE STUFFING

Mix together the chicken, creamed spinach, tomatoes, onion, cheese, and egg in a medium bowl. Set aside.

Step 3: COOK PASTA

Bring a large stock pot of water to boil; season with salt. Stir in the pasta shells; cook for 8 to 10 minutes, or until al dente. Drain.

Step 4: ASSEMBLE AND BAKE

Pour half the Alfredo sauce in the casserole. Stuff the cooked shells with filling. Arrange shells in the casserole. Pour the remaining sauce over the shells and sprinkle with cheese. Cover and bake for 20 minutes or until heated through and the cheese is golden.

COOKS NOTES: If you can't locate Boursin, chive and garlic-flavored cream cheese makes a delicious substitution.

• MAKES 4-6 SERVINGS •

Warm Cranberry-Jalapeño Compote Chicken

Sweet cranberries combine deliciously with the heat of the jalapeño in this easy meal.

2	tablespoons canola oil
2	tablespoons butter
2	cups frozen diced onion
2	teaspoons minced garlic
2	cups dried cranberries
1	small jalapeño, stem removed, seeded and minced
1	cup white wine
½	cup loosely packed cilantro, chopped
1	rotisserie chicken, carved into 8 pieces, warm
1	green onion, thinly sliced

Step 1: SWEAT ONIONS

Place the oil and butter in a large skillet over medium heat; stir in the onion. Cook, stirring frequently, for 4 to 6 minutes or until onions are translucent. Stir in the garlic; cook 1 minute more.

Step 2: FINISH COMPOTE

Stir in the cranberries, jalapeño, and wine. Reduce the heat to low and simmer until the liquid is reduced by half. Stir in the cilantro.

Step 3: ASSEMBLE

Arrange the chicken on a serving platter. Pour the compote over the chicken and sprinkle with green onion. Serve hot.

COOKS NOTES: This is delicious served with plain, jasmine, or basmati rice on the side.

• MAKES 4-6 SERVINGS •

Emperor's Fried Rice

Much better than take out, this fried rice is fit for a king!

4	tablespoons butter, divided
3	tablespoons sesame oil
6	cups cold cooked rice (a few days old is best!)
2	green onions, thinly sliced on the bias
1	teaspoon minced roasted garlic
2	cups frozen peas and carrots, thawed
1	cup diced rotisserie chicken
1	4-ounce can tiny shrimp, rinsed and drained
1	cup diced cooked pork (leftover tenderloin, roast or chops are great)
2	large eggs
3	tablespoons milk
	Soy sauce, to taste
	Ground white pepper to taste
¼	cup loosely packed cilantro, chopped

Step 1: COOK RICE

Place 3 tablespoons of butter and the sesame oil in a wok or large skillet over medium high heat. Stir in the rice onions, garlic, peas and carrots, chicken, shrimp, and pork. Cook, stirring often, for 6 to 8 minutes or until heated through.

Step 2: COOK THE EGGS

Push the fried rice to the side to make room for the eggs. Add the remaining butter. Beat the eggs and milk in a small bowl; pour into the wok. Cook, breaking up the eggs into small pieces as it cooks. Cook for 2 to 3 minutes or until just set but not dry.

Step 3: COMBINE AND SEASON

Mix the eggs into the fried rice. Check the seasoning, adding soy sauce and ground pepper as needed.

Step 4: GARNISH AND SERVE

Pile the fried rice onto a serving platter. Sprinkle with cilantro and serve.

• MAKES 4-6 SERVINGS •

Gingered Peach Chicken and Rice

Sweet and sour taste with just a touch of heat.

1	tablespoon butter
1	tablespoon canola oil
1	to 2 shallots, minced
2	large peaches, peeled, pitted and diced
1	cup sugar peas, trimmed
2	cups coarsely shredded rotisserie chicken
2	teaspoons rice vinegar
¼	cup peach preserves
1	teaspoon fresh grated ginger
	Pinch red pepper flakes
4	cups cooked jasmine or basmati rice
1	small bunch chives, sliced thin

Step 1: SWEAT SHALLOTS

Place the butter and oil in a large skillet over medium heat; add the shallots. Cook, stirring occasionally, for 3 to 4 minutes or until translucent. Add the peaches and peas; continue cooking for 4 to 5 minutes or until the peaches just begin to soften. Stir in the chicken.

Step 2: MAKE SAUCE

Stir in the rice vinegar, peach preserves, ginger, and red pepper flakes. Reduce the heat to low; simmer 10 minutes.

Step 3: PLATE AND SERVE

Mound the hot cooked rice in the center of a serving platter. Top with the Gingered Peach Chicken. Sprinkle with chives and serve.

COOKS NOTES: Nectarines make a terrific substitution for the peaches.

• MAKES 4 SERVINGS •

Fettuccine with Creamy Vodka Chicken Sauce

This sauce is so vibrant and delicious; fresh basil really makes it special.

1	tablespoons olive oil
1	tablespoons butter
1	cup frozen diced onion
2	teaspoons minced garlic
1	28-ounce can chef's cut tomatoes (strips)
½	cup loosely packed basil, chopped
1	green onion, sliced thin
½	cup vodka
2	cups diced rotisserie chicken
2	cups whipping cream
	Kosher salt to taste
	Ground black pepper to taste
12	ounces fettuccine
½	cup grated Parmesan cheese

Step 1: SWEAT ONIONS

Place the oil and butter in a large saucepan over medium heat; stir in the onion. Cook, stirring frequently, for 3 to 4 minutes or until the onion is translucent. Stir in the garlic, tomatoes, basil, and onion. Cook, stirring frequently, for 2 to 3 minutes.

Step 2: ADD VODKA

Remove the pan from the heat; pour in the vodka. Return to the heat and carefully ignite the vodka. Once the flames are extinguished, stir in the chicken. Simmer for 10 minutes.

Step 3: FINISH SAUCE

Stir the whipping cream into the sauce. Reduce the heat to low and cook, stirring occasionally, for 8 to 10 minutes or until thickened. Check the seasoning, adding salt and ground pepper as needed.

Step 4: COOK PASTA

While the sauce is simmering, bring a large stock pot of water to a boil. Stir in the pasta and cook for 8 to 10 minutes or until al dente. Drain.

Step 5: GARNISH AND SERVE

Place the fettuccine on a large serving platter; pour the sauce over the pasta. Sprinkle with Parmesan; serve.

• MAKES 4-6 SERVINGS •

❊   ❊   ❊   ❊   ❊

Pineapple-Rum Chicken and Rice Bake

This one dish meal is a tropical take on sweet and sour chicken.

2	cups uncooked long grain white rice
2	cups chicken broth
1	20-ounce can crushed pineapple
1	cup rum
1	10-ounce jar prepared sweet and sour sauce
½	cup loosely packed cilantro, chopped
1	whole rotisserie chicken, cut into 8 pieces
½	cup cashew halves

Step 1: PREHEAT OVEN

Preheat the oven to 350° F.

Step 2: ASSEMBLE INGREDIENTS

Mix together the rice, broth, pineapple, rum, sweet and sour sauce, and cilantro in a covered 3-quart casserole dish. Arrange the chicken over the rice. Cover.

Step 3: BAKE

Bake in the preheated oven for 20 to 25 minutes or until the liquid is absorbed and the rice is cooked through. Remove the cover; sprinkle with cashews. Cook for an additional 10 to 15 minutes or until the cashews are lightly golden.

• MAKES 6-8 SERVINGS •

Hunter Style Chicken

Classic, slow roasted flavor in a flash!

2	tablespoons olive oil
2	tablespoons butter
1	cup frozen diced onion
1	8-ounce package sliced mushrooms
½	cup red wine
2	cups chicken broth
2	14.5-ounce can diced Italian seasoned tomatoes
1	teaspoon finely chopped fresh oregano leaves
1	teaspoon finely chopped fresh flat leaf parsley
1	whole rotisserie chicken, carved into 8 pieces

Step 1: PREHEAT OVEN AND PREPARE CASSEROLE DISH

Preheat the oven to 350° F. Spray a 3-quart casserole dish with cooking spray.

Step 2: START SAUCE

Place the oil and butter in a large saucepan over medium heat; stir in the onion. Cook for 4 to 6 minutes or until translucent. Stir in the mushrooms; cook for 4 to 6 minutes or until the edges of the mushrooms begin to brown.

Step 3: FINISH SAUCE

Pour the wine into the saucepan. Stir constantly, taking care to scrap the bits off the bottom of the pan. Stir in the broth and tomatoes. Reduce the heat to low. Continue to cook, stirring occasionally, for 15 minutes or until reduced by half. Stir in the oregano and parsley.

Step 4: SAUCE THE CHICKEN

Place the chicken pieces in the prepared casserole dish. Pour the sauce over the chicken. Cover and bake for 15 minutes. Serve hot.

COOKS NOTES: Serve with roasted potatoes, carrots, and parsnips for a hearty meal.

• MAKES 6-8 SERVINGS •

Lemon-Basil Chicken Pilaf

Lemon and basil infused rice raises the bar on pilaf. No longer relegated to side dish status, this pilaf is the star of the meal!

2	tablespoons olive oil
2	tablespoons butter
1	cup frozen diced onion
1	small carrot, grated
2	cups uncooked long grain rice
½	cup orzo
2	teaspoons minced garlic
1	teaspoon lemon zest
2	cups diced rotisserie chicken
5	cups chicken broth
½	cup loosely packed basil leaves, chopped

Step 1: SWEAT VEGETABLES

Place the oil and butter in a large saucepan over medium heat. Stir in the onion and carrot; cook, stirring frequently, for 3 to 4 minutes or until the onions are translucent.

Step 2: COOK RICE AND ORZO

Stir the rice and orzo into the vegetables. Cook, stirring frequently, for 4 to 6 minutes or until it starts to smell nutty.

Step 3: ADD THE CHICKEN AND BROTH

Stir in the garlic, lemon zest, chicken, and broth. Bring to a boil, stirring occasionally. Cover, reduce the heat to low, and cook for 20 to 25 minutes or until the liquid is absorbed and the rice is tender.

Step 4: ADD BASIL AND SERVE

Stir in the basil. Pour onto a serving platter and serve.

COOKS NOTES: To complete this meal, serve with a garden salad and bread.

• MAKES 4-6 SERVINGS •

Middle Eastern Chicken Bowls

Pungent spices infuse the chicken in this savory dish.

2	tablespoons olive oil
1	cup frozen diced onions
½	cup shredded carrots
2	teaspoons minced garlic
2	cups coarsely shredded rotisserie chicken
3	cups chicken broth
1	teaspoon smoked paprika
1	teaspoon ground cumin
½	teaspoon ground coriander
¼	teaspoon ground cinnamon
½	cup golden raisins
¼	cup dried apricots, sliced
4	to 6 fresh figs, quartered and stems removed
½	cup loosely packed cilantro, chopped
1	teaspoon lemon juice
	Kosher salt to taste
	Ground black pepper to taste
8	cups cooked basmati rice
½	cup slivered almonds, toasted
1	green onion, sliced

Step 1: SWEAT VEGETABLES

Pour the oil into a large skillet over medium heat; stir in the onions and carrots. Cook, stirring frequently for 3 to 4 minutes, or until the onions are translucent. Stir in the garlic; cook for 1 minute more.

Step 2: ADD CHICKEN AND SIMMER

Stir in the chicken, broth, paprika, cumin, coriander, and cinnamon. Reduce the heat to low; simmer for 15 minutes.

Step 3: ADD FRUIT

Stir in the raisins, apricots, figs, cilantro, and lemon juice. Cook, stirring occasionally, for 10 minutes. Check the seasoning, adding salt and pepper as needed.

Step 4: GARNISH AND SERVE

Mound the rice in 4 individual serving bowls. Spoon the chicken mixture evenly over the 4 bowls of rice. Sprinkle with almonds and green onion; serve hot.

COOKS NOTES: This chicken is also delicious served over a mound of couscous.

• MAKES 4 SERVINGS •

Moroccan Chicken

Traditional Moroccan chicken is stewed in a tagine for hours...this one's done in less than one.

3	tablespoons olive oil
2	cups frozen diced onion
1	cup frozen sliced carrots, thawed
1	15-ounce can garbanzo beans, rinsed and drained
2	cups chicken broth
2	teaspoons minced garlic
1	teaspoon ground cumin
1/2	teaspoon fresh ground cinnamon
1	teaspoon ground sweet Hungarian paprika
1	teaspoon hot sauce
	Juice of 1 lemon
1/2	teaspoon white ground pepper
1	tablespoon honey
1	preserved lemon, chopped
1/2	cup pitted green olives
6	cups cooked couscous, warm
1	rotisserie chicken, cut into 8 pieces
	Kosher salt to taste
	Ground black pepper to taste
1	teaspoon chopped fresh flat-leaf parsley, chopped
1	teaspoon chopped cilantro
1	teaspoon chopped mint

Step 1: SWEAT VEGETABLES

Pour the oil in a large Dutch oven or stock pot over medium heat; stir in the onions and carrots. Cook, stirring frequently, for 4 to 6 minutes

Step 2: ADD BEANS AND BROTH

Stir in the beans, broth, garlic, cumin, cinnamon, paprika, hot sauce, lemon juice, pepper, honey, preserved lemon, and olives. Reduce the heat to low and simmer for 15 minutes.

Step 3: ADD CHICKEN

Place the chicken pieces over the bean mixture. Cover and simmer for 10 minutes more.

Step 4: GARNISH AND SERVE

Mound the couscous on a large serving platter; arrange the chicken on top of the couscous. Check the seasoning of the bean mixture, adding salt and pepper as needed; Pour over chicken. Sprinkle with chopped herbs and serve hot.

COOKS NOTES: Preserved lemons can be found in specialty food stores.

• MAKES 6-8 SERVINGS •

One-Pot Chicken Spaghetti

Spaghetti made quickly—and only one pot to wash after dinner…perfect!

2	tablespoons olive oil
1	cup frozen diced onions
1	8-ounce package sliced mushrooms
1	1-pound, 10-ounce jar garden style spaghetti sauce
2	cups coarsely shredded rotisserie chicken
2	cups chicken broth
8	ounces spaghetti, broken in half
½	cup loosely packed basil leaves, chopped
1	cup grated Parmesan cheese

Step 1: SWEAT VEGETABLES

Pour the olive oil, onions, and mushrooms in a large stock pot over medium heat. Cook, stirring occasionally, for 4 to 6 minutes or until the onions are translucent.

Step 2: START SAUCE

Stir in the spaghetti sauce, chicken, and broth. Bring to a boil, stirring occasionally.

Step 3: COOK SPAGHETTI

Stir in the spaghetti, a little at a time, stirring constantly. Reduce the heat to low heat. Cover and simmer for 15 to 20 minutes, stirring frequently, until the spaghetti is al dente. Stir in the basil.

Step 3: GARNISH AND SERVE

Pile the spaghetti into a large, shallow serving bowl. Sprinkle with cheese and serve.

COOKS NOTES: For a complete Italian meal, serve with garlic bread and a crisp garden salad.

• MAKES 4-6 SERVINGS •

Presto Pesto Chicken Penne

Get dinner on the table in 15 minutes with this fast and fabulous recipe.

	Kosher salt to taste
8	ounces penne
2	tablespoons olive oil
3	tablespoons prepared pesto
¼	cup heavy cream
	Ground black pepper to taste
2	cups coarsely shredded rotisserie chicken, warm
½	cup grated Parmesan cheese
¼	cup toasted pine nuts

Step 1: COOK PASTA

Bring a large stock pot of water to a boil over medium high heat; season with salt. Add the penne; cook for 9 to 12 minutes or until al dente. Drain, reserving ½ cup of the cooking water. Place in a large serving bowl.

Step 2: SAUCE PASTA

Toss the olive oil, pesto, heavy cream, and salt and pepper to taste into the penne. Add cooking water as needed to make the sauce. Add chicken and toss.

Step 3: GARNISH AND SERVE

Sprinkle Parmesan and pine nuts over the pasta; serve.

COOKS NOTES: Toss in some strips of marinated sun-dried tomatoes for a blast of flavor and color.

• MAKES 4 SERVINGS •

Orange-Ginger Sesame Chicken Rice Bowl

Add chopsticks and fortune cookies to complete the Asian theme.

3	tablespoons sesame oil
2	cups frozen bell pepper and onion mix
3	tablespoons seasoned rice vinegar
½	prepared orange marmalade
½	teaspoon fresh grated ginger
	Pinch red pepper flakes
1	11-ounce can mandarin orange segments, drained
2	cups coarsely shredded rotisserie chicken
8	cups hot cooked white rice
2	tablespoons toasted sesame seeds
1	green onion, thinly sliced on the bias

Step 1: START ORANGE-GINGER SAUCE

Pour the oil in a large saucepan over medium heat; stir in the bell pepper mix. Cook, stirring frequently, for 4 to 6 minutes or until the onions are translucent. Stir in the rice vinegar, orange marmalade, ginger, and red pepper flakes.

Step 2: ADD CHICKEN AND ORANGES

Stir the orange segments and chicken into the sauce; bring to a boil. Reduce the heat to low; simmer, stirring occasionally, for 10 minutes.

Step 3: ASSEMBLE AND SERVE

Divide the cooked rice into 4 individual serving bowls; top with an equal portion of the chicken mixture. Sprinkle with sesame seeds and green onion and serve.

COOKS NOTES: For added color and flavor, toss in broccoli florets along with the bell pepper mix.

• MAKES 4 SERVINGS •

Quick Chicken Paprikash

So rich and flavorful you'll think it's been simmering all day.

1	tablespoon canola oil
4	sliced bacon, diced
2	cups frozen bell pepper and onion mix
2	teaspoons minced garlic
1	28-ounce can crushed tomatoes
1	cup chicken broth
2	tablespoons Hungarian paprika
	Several drops of Tabasco sauce, to taste
1	whole rotisserie chicken, cut into 8 pieces
1	cup sour cream
6	cups cooked white rice, warm
1	green onion, sliced

Step 1: SWEAT VEGETABLES

Pour the canola oil in a large Dutch oven over medium heat. Stir in the bacon; cook, stirring constantly, for 3 to 4 minutes or until the bacon begins to get crispy. Stir in the bell peppers and onion mix. Cook, stirring frequently, for 4 to 6 minutes or until the onions are translucent. Add the garlic and cook 1 minute longer. Stir in the tomatoes, broth, paprika, and Tabasco sauce; Bring to a boil.

Step 2: ADD CHICKEN

Arrange the chicken parts in the sauce; return to a boil. Reduce the heat to low; simmer for 20 minutes or until heated through.

Step 3: FINISH SAUCE

Gently remove the chicken to a plate. Stir the sour cream into the paprikash sauce. Return the chicken to the pot. Cover and simmer for 10 minutes.

Step 4: GARNISH AND SERVE

Mound the cooked rice onto a large serving platter. Arrange the chicken over the rice; pour the sauce over the chicken. Sprinkle with green onion and serve.

• MAKES 6-8 SERVINGS •

Quick Coq au Vin

Traditional chicken and wine is slow roasted…using rotisserie chicken jump starts the process!

2	tablespoons butter
2	tablespoons canola oil
1	16-ounce package frozen pearl onions
2	cups baby peeled carrots
4	cups baby red potatoes
2	teaspoons minced garlic
1	teaspoon dried marjoram
1	whole rotisserie chicken, carved into 8 parts
2	cups white wine
1	cup chicken broth
¼	cup loosely packed flat leaf parsley, chopped

Step 1: SWEAT VEGETABLES

Place the butter and canola in a large Dutch oven over medium heat. Stir in the onions, carrots and potatoes. Cook, stirring occasionally, for 4 to 5 minutes or until the onions are translucent. Stir in the garlic and marjoram; cook for 1 minute more.

Step 2: ADD CHICKEN AND SIMMER

Arrange the chicken over the vegetables. Pour the wine and broth over the chicken. Bring to a boil. Cover and reduce the heat to low. Simmer for 15 minutes. Remove the cover and continue simmering 10 minutes longer, or until the vegetables are tender.

Step 3: GARNISH AND SERVE

Sprinkle with parsley and serve.

COOKS NOTES: A crisp garden salad and loaf of crusty French bread complete this meal.

• MAKES 6-8 SERVINGS •

Rápida Chicken Tamale Pies

Prepared polenta gets this Latin favorite on the table in no time!

1	cup diced rotisserie chicken
1	cup frozen Southwest style corn (with onions and bell peppers)
¼	cup loosely packed cilantro, chopped
1	2.25-ounce can sliced olives, reserve 4 slices for garnish
1	cup prepared salsa
2	cups shredded Cheddar cheese, divided
8	¼-inch slices from a 1-pound tube of prepared polenta
4	tablespoons sour cream

Step 1: PREHEAT OVEN AND PREPARE RAMEKINS

Preheat the oven to 350° F. Spray the insides of four 1-cup capacity ramekins or au gratin dishes with cooking spray; set aside.

Step 2: MIX TAMALE FILLING

Mix together the chicken, corn mix, cilantro, olives, salsa, and 1½ cups of cheese in a medium bowl.

Step 3: ASSEMBLE AND BAKE

Place 1 slice of polenta on the bottom of each ramekin. Evenly divide the tamale filling among each of the ramekins, packing gently. Top with a slice of polenta and sprinkle with some of the remaining cheese. Bake in a preheated oven for 20 minutes or until bubbling and the cheese is lighly golden. Rest for 5 minutes.

Step 4: GARNISH AND SERVE

Place a dollop of sour cream and a slice of olive on top of each tamale pie. Serve hot.

COOKS NOTES: Kick up the heat by using hot salsa. Serve with Spanish style rice and refried beans for a complete fiesta!

• MAKES 4 SERVINGS •

Indian Butter Chicken

Exotic spices transport you to India with every bite!

2	tablespoons butter
1	tablespoon peanut oil
½	cup frozen diced onion
1	teaspoon grated ginger
1	teaspoon minced garlic
1	teaspoon chili powder
1	teaspoon ground cumin
¼	teaspoon cayenne pepper, or more to taste
2	teaspoons lemon juice
1	28-ounce can crushed tomatoes
1	cup chicken broth
1	bay leaf
3	cups diced rotisserie chicken
1	teaspoon garam masala
¼	cup plain yogurt
1	cup half and half
	Kosher salt to taste
	Ground black pepper to taste
6	cups cooked basmati rice
¼	cup loosely packed cilantro, chopped

Step 1: MAKE SAUCE

Place the butter and peanut oil in a large saucepan over medium heat. Add the onion; cook for 3 to 4 minutes or until translucent. Stir in the ginger, garlic, chili powder, cumin, cayenne pepper, lemon juice, crushed tomatoes, chicken broth, bay leaf, and chicken. Bring to boil, stirring occasionally. Reduce the heat to low; simmer for 15 minutes.

Step 2: FINISH SAUCE

Remove the bay leaf; stir in the garam masala, yogurt, and half and half. Simmer for 10 minutes or until thickened. Check the seasoning, adding salt and pepper as needed.

Step 3: GARNISH AND SERVE

Mound the cooked rice onto a serving platter. Pour the sauced chicken over the top of the rice, sprinkle with cilantro, and serve.

• MAKES 4-6 SERVINGS •

⌗   ⌗   ⌗

Athens Chicken Pizza

Simple ingredients, huge flavor!

1	6-ounce jar marinated artichoke hearts
4	6- to 8-inch diameter loaves flatbread
2	cups diced rotisserie chicken
½	cup pitted and sliced kalamata olives
4	sun-dried tomatoes, cut into strips
1	green onion, sliced
¼	cup loosely packed oregano, chopped
1	cup crumbled feta cheese

Step 1: PREHEAT OVEN

Preheat the oven to 400° F.

Step 2: ASSEMBLE PIZZA

Place the artichoke hearts and marinade in a food processor; pulse for 10 to 15 seconds or until coarsely puréed. Spread artichoke purée to within 1 inch of each flatbread edge. Top each flatbread with one fourth of each of the following: chicken, olives, tomatoes, green onion, oregano, and cheese.

Step 4: BAKE AND SERVE

Place on an ungreased baking sheet; bake in the preheated oven for 10 to 12 minutes or until the cheese is melted. Rest for 10 minutes. Cut into wedges and serve.

• MAKES 4 SERVINGS •

BBQ Chicken Stuffed Pizza

Stuffed is right…stuffed with full bodied flavors.

2	approximately 1-pound each prepared pizza crust doughs
2	cups shredded Italian cheese blend
5	Roma tomatoes, thinly sliced
3	cups diced rotisserie chicken
1	cup prepared barbecue sauce
½	cup diced red onion
½	cup loosely packed cilantro, chopped
2	tablespoons olive oil
¼	cup Parmesan cheese

Step 1: PREHEAT OVEN AND PREPARE PAN

Preheat the oven to 350° F. Spray a baking sheet with cooking spray.

Step 2: ASSEMBLE PIZZA

Press 1 portion of pizza dough into a 12-inch circle on the prepared baking sheet. Arrange the cheese to within 1 inch of the edge, followed by the tomato slices, then the chicken. Drizzle with barbecue sauce; sprinkle with onion and cilantro. Press the remaining portion of pizza dough into a 12-inch circle, carefully lay over the pizza. Roll the edges up and crimp to seal well. Brush with olive oil; sprinkle with Parmesan cheese.

Step 3: BAKE AND SERVE

Bake the pizza in the preheated oven for 30 to 40 minutes or until crust is golden. Rest for 10 minutes. Cut into wedges and serve.

• MAKES 6-8 SERVINGS •

Thai Chicken Pizza

Creamy green curry sauce with just the right amount of heat will have your taste buds begging for more.

1	13.5-ounce can coconut milk
1	teaspoon green curry paste
1	about 1-pound prepared pizza crust dough
2	cups baby spinach, chopped
1½	cups diced rotisserie chicken
1	small red bell pepper, pared, seeded and cut into thin strips
1	green onion, sliced
¼	cup loosely packed Thai basil leaves, chopped
2	cups shredded mozzarella cheese
½	cup chopped peanuts

Step 1: MAKE SAUCE

Pour the coconut milk in a medium saucepan over medium heat. Stir in the green curry paste. Simmer, stirring occasionally, until the sauce has reduced by about half.

Step 2: PREHEAT OVEN AND PREPARE PAN

Preheat the oven to 400° F. Lightly grease a 12- to 14-inch pizza pan or baking sheet with cooking spray.

Step 3: ASSEMBLE PIZZA

Press the pizza crust dough onto the prepared pan. Spread the sauce to within 1 inch of the pizza edge. Top the pizza with spinach, chicken, bell pepper, green onion, Thai basil, and cheese. Sprinkle with peanuts.

Step 4: BAKE AND SERVE

Bake the pizza in the preheated oven for 12 to 15 minutes or until the cheese is melted and lightly golden. Rest for 10 minutes. Cut into wedges and serve.

COOKS NOTES: Fresh pizza dough is available in the dairy case of most markets, although a 1-pound frozen bread dough loaf makes a nice substitution.

• MAKES 4-6 SERVINGS •

Red Curry Pineapple Chicken with Rice

Red curry provides just the right amount of zest for this sweet and spicy dish.

3	tablespoons sesame oil
4	cups frozen bell pepper and onion mix
2	13.5-ounce cans coconut milk
1	tablespoon red curry paste
2	tablespoons fish sauce
1	8-ounce can pineapple chunks, drained
2	cups shredded rotisserie chicken
¼	cup cold water
2	heaping tablespoons cornstarch
1	cup whole cashews
	Kosher salt to taste
	Ground white pepper to taste
6	cups cooked jasmine rice, warm
¼	cup loosely packed cilantro, chopped

Step 1: SWEAT PEPPERS AND ONIONS

Pour the oil into a large saucepan over medium heat. Stir in the bell pepper and onions; cook for 4 to 6 minutes or until just softened.

Step 2: MAKE SAUCE

Stir in the coconut milk, red curry, fish sauce, pineapple and chicken. Bring to a boil. Reduce the heat to low heat; simmer for 15 minutes.

Step 3: THICKEN SAUCE

Whisk together the water and cornstarch. Stir slurry into the sauce. Cook, stirring constantly, for 4 to 6 minutes or until smooth and thickened. Stir in the cashews. Check the seasoning, adding red curry paste, salt, and pepper as needed.

Step 4: GARNISH AND SERVE

Mound rice on a serving platter; top with chicken mixture. Sprinkle with cilantro and serve.

• MAKES 4-6 SERVINGS •

Spicy Chicken Broccolini Lo-Mein

This Asian inspired meal is quick and easy enough for a weeknight supper.

2	tablespoons sesame oil
2	tablespoons canola oil
2	teaspoon minced garlic
1	teaspoon grated ginger
1	pound broccolini, cut into diagonal, bite sized pieces
2	green onions, cut into 2 inch lengths, on the bias
1	cup chicken broth
¼	cup hoisin sauce
¼	cup soy sauce
½	teaspoon red pepper flakes
2	cups coarsely shredded rotisserie chicken
4	cups cooked Chinese noodles
3	tablespoons toasted sesame seeds

Step 1: COOK GARLIC AND GINGER

Pour the sesame and canola oils into a wok or large skillet over medium high heat; add the garlic and ginger. Cook, stirring frequently, for 1 to 2 minutes or until just golden.

Step 2: ADD BROCCOLINI AND ONIONS

Stir in the broccolini and onions; cook, stirring frequently, for 2 to 3 minutes or until just beginning to soften. Stir in the broth, hoisin sauce, soy sauce, and red pepper flakes. Cook for another 3 to 4 minutes or until the broccolini is crisp-tender.

Step 3: ADD CHICKEN AND NOODLES

Stir in the chicken and noodles. Cook, stirring frequently, for 3 to 4 minutes or until heated through.

Step 4: GARNISH AND SERVE

Mound Spicy Chicken Broccolini Lo-Mein onto a serving platter. Sprinkle with sesame seeds and serve.

• MAKES 4-6 SERVINGS •

Weeknight Chicken and Dumplings

Home cooked goodness with fast food timing!

2	tablespoons butter
2	tablespoons olive oil
2	cups frozen diced onions
2	cups baby peeled carrots
2	ribs celery, diced
2	teaspoons minced garlic
1/4	cup all-purpose flour
6	cups chicken broth
2	cups frozen Southern style hash browns
3	cups large chunks rotisserie chicken
1	bay leaf
2	teaspoons fresh thyme
1/2	cut heavy cream
	Kosher salt to taste
	Ground black pepper to taste
1 1/2	cups packaged buttermilk biscuit mix
3	tablespoons snipped fresh chives
1	large egg, beaten
1/4	cup whole milk

Step 1: SWEAT VEGETABLES

Place the butter and olive oil in a large Dutch oven over medium high heat. Add the onions, carrots, celery, and garlic; cook for 4 to 5 or until the onions are translucent.

Step 2: CREATE SAUCE

Sprinkle the flour evenly over the vegetables. Cook, stirring constantly, for 2 to 3 minutes or until the flour is golden. Slowly pour in the chicken broth, stirring constantly until thickened. Stir in the hash browns, chicken, bay leaf, and thyme; reduce the heat to low. Simmer for 15 minutes. Stir in the cream. Check the seasoning, adding salt and pepper as needed. Discard the bay leaf.

Step 3: MAKE DUMPLINGS

Mix together the biscuit mix and chives in a medium bowl. Stir in the egg and milk, mixing until batter just comes together—don't over mix. Drop by heaping tablespoonfuls over the simmering chicken. Cover; cook for 10 minutes. Remove the lid and continue to cook for 10 minutes or until the dumplings are light and fluffy. Serve hot.

• MAKES 6-8 SERVINGS •

❊   ❊   ❊

Minute Stroganoff with Chicken

Creamy and satisfying, this stroganoff is a perfect weeknight meal.

2	tablespoons butter
2	tablespoons canola oil
1	8-ounce package sliced mushrooms
1	12-ounce jar mushroom gravy
2	cups frozen peas, thawed
2	cups coarsely shredded rotisserie chicken
8	ounces egg noodles
1	cup sour cream
	Kosher salt to taste
	Ground white pepper to taste

Step 1: COOK MUSHROOMS

Place the butter and oil in a large saucepan over medium heat; stir in the mushrooms. Cook, stirring occasionally, for 4 to 6 minutes or until the edges begin to brown. Stir in the gravy, peas, and chicken. Bring to a boil; reduce the heat to low and simmer for 10 minutes.

Step 2: COOK NOODLES

Bring a large stockpot of water to boil; season with salt. Stir in the egg noodles. Cook for 9 to 12 minutes or until tender. Drain.

Step 3: FINISH AND ASSEMBLE

Stir the noodles and sour cream into the chicken mixture. Check the seasoning, adding salt and pepper as needed. Place in a large serving bowl; serve hot.

• MAKES 6-8 SERVINGS •

Stuffed Eggplant

Savory chicken filling with just the right amount of basil make these special enough for company and easy enough for everyday!

4	Japanese eggplants
3	tablespoons olive oil, divided
1/2	cup frozen diced onion
2	teaspoons minced garlic
2	cups diced rotisserie chicken
4	sun-dried tomatoes packed in oil, minced
1/2	cup loosely packed basil leaves, chopped
1	cup shredded mozzarella
1/4	cup grated Parmesan cheese

Step 1: PREHEAT OVEN AND PREPARE PAN

Preheat the oven to 350° F. Spray a 9x13 baking pan with cooking spray.

Step 2: PREPARE EGGPLANTS

Pierce the eggplants several times with a fork; place in a microwave safe dish. Cook on high for 4 to 6 minutes or until softened. When cool enough to handle, make a deep slit lengthwise down each eggplant. Set aside.

Step 3: MAKE FILLING

Pour the oil in a large skillet over medium heat. Stir in the onion and garlic; cook, stirring frequently, for 1 to 2 minutes or until the garlic is just golden. Remove from the heat. Stir in the chicken, tomatoes, and basil. Let cool for 5 minutes; stir in the mozzarella.

Step 4: STUFF AND BAKE

Place the eggplants onto the prepared baking pan. Stuff each eggplant with one fourth of the filling. Sprinkle each with 1 tablespoon Parmesan. Bake in the preheated oven for 20 to 30 minutes or until the cheese is golden.

• MAKES 4 SERVINGS •

CASSEROLES

Chicken-Artichoke Casserole

Gruyere and Asiago cheeses are complimented by marinated artichokes in this creamy casserole.

¼	cup butter
3	tablespoons minced onion
¼	cup all-purpose flour
3	cups whole milk
1	cup shredded Gruyere cheese
1	cup shredded Asiago cheese, divided
2	cups shredded rotisserie chicken
1	6.5-ounce jar marinated artichoke hearts, chopped and liquid reserved
	Kosher salt to taste
	Ground white pepper to taste
2	cups uncooked small pasta shells or bowties

Step 1: PREHEAT OVEN AND PREPARE CASSEROLE DISH

Preheat the oven to 350° F. Spray a 2-quart casserole dish with cooking spray.

Step 2: BEGIN SAUCE

Melt the butter in a large saucepan over medium heat. Stir in the minced onion; cook for 1 minute. Add the flour; cook, stirring constantly, for 4 to 6 minutes or until lightly golden. Stir in the milk. Cook, whisking constantly, for 8 to 10 minutes or until thick and creamy. Reduce the heat to low. Stir in the gruyere, ½ cup of Asiago cheese, chicken, artichoke hearts and reserved liquid, salt, and pepper to taste.

Step 3: COOK PASTA

Bring a large pot of water to boil over medium high heat; season with salt. Stir in the pasta; cook for 5 minutes. The pasta will be undercooked. Drain.

Step 4: ASSEMBLE & BAKE

Stir the pasta into the cheese sauce. Pour into the prepared casserole; sprinkle with the remaining Asiago cheese. Bake for 40 to 50 minutes or until hot and golden. Rest for 10 minutes before serving.

• MAKES 6-8 SERVINGS •

Baked Creamy Chicken Sofrito Penne

Baked macaroni and cheese kicked up...way up!

	Kosher salt to taste
8	ounces penne
2	cups coarsely shredded rotisserie chicken
2	12-ounce jars prepared Spanish sofrito
1	cup chicken broth
1	cup Crema Mexicana
½	cup loosely packed cilantro leaves, chopped
2	cups shredded pepper jack cheese

Step 1: PREHEAT OVEN AND PREPARE CASSEROLE DISH

Preheat the oven to 350° F. Spray a 2-quart casserole dish with cooking spray.

Step 2: COOK PASTA

Bring a large stockpot three fourths full of water to a boil; lightly season with kosher salt. Stir in the penne. Cook for 4 to 5 minutes. The pasta should be very undercooked. Drain.

Step 3: MAKE SAUCE

Stir together the chicken, sofrito, chicken broth, Crema Mexicana, and cooked penne.

Step 4: ASSEMBLE CASSEROLE

Pour half the sauced penne in the casserole dish; sprinkle with half the cilantro and half the cheese. Pour in the remaining penne, followed by the remaining cilantro and remaining cheese.

Step 5: BAKE

Bake for 10 to 15 minutes or until the penne is tender but firm and the cheese is melted.

• MAKES 4-6 SERVINGS •

Curried Chicken Casserole

Spicy curry is a perfect partner with chicken, peas, and potatoes in this crowd pleaser.

3	tablespoons canola oil
1	cup frozen diced onion
1	teaspoon grated fresh ginger root
2	teaspoons minced garlic
3	tablespoons curry powder
½	teaspoon ground cinnamon
2	teaspoons paprika
1	14.5-ounce can diced tomatoes
4	cups frozen Southern style hash brown potatoes, thawed
2	cups frozen peas
3	cups diced rotisserie chicken
1	13.5-ounce can coconut milk
1	cup plain yogurt
2	teaspoons lemon juice
	Kosher salt to taste
	Ground white pepper to taste
1	cup shredded coconut

Step 1: PREHEAT OVEN AND PREPARE CASSEROLE DISH

Preheat the oven to 350° F. Spray a 2-quart casserole dish with cooking spray.

Step 2: SWEAT ONIONS

Pour the oil in a large saucepan over medium heat; stir in the onion, ginger, garlic, curry powder, cinnamon, and paprika. Cook, stirring constantly, for 2 to 3 minutes or until the onions are translucent and the spices are fragrant.

Step 3: FINISH FILLING

Stir in the tomatoes, potatoes, peas, chicken, coconut milk, yogurt, and lemon juice. Check the seasoning, adding salt and pepper as needed.

Step 4: ASSEMBLE AND BAKE

Pour the mixture into the prepared casserole; top with coconut. Bake for 30 to 40 minutes, or until the coconut is golden brown.

COOKS NOTES: Speed up the thawing of the hash browns by placing them in a microwave safe dish and cover with water. Heat on high power for 5 to 7 minutes or until thawed; drain.

• MAKES 6-8 SERVINGS •

Bianco Lasagna

White asparagus adds elegance to this special lasagna.

	Kosher salt to taste
	Kosher salt to taste
9	lasagna noodles
2	16-ounce jars prepared alfredo sauce
	Ground nutmeg, to taste
2	tablespoons chopped fresh flat leaf parsley
1	15-ounce container cottage cheese
2	cups diced rotisserie chicken
1	cup grated Parmesan cheese, divided
1	pound thin white asparagus tips
1	8-ounce package sliced white mushrooms
1	10-ounce package frozen cauliflower florets, thawed
2	cups shredded mozzarella cheese, divided

Step 1: PREHEAT OVEN AND PREPARE CASSEROLE DISH

Preheat the oven to 350° F. Spray a 9x13 casserole dish with cooking spray.

Step 2: COOK PASTA

Bring a large stock pot of water to a boil over medium high heat; season with salt. Stir in the lasagna noodles; cook for 7 to 9 minutes or until al dente. Drain, place in a medium bowl, and coat with 1 tablespoon of olive oil.

Step 3: ASSEMBLE LASAGNA

Spread enough alfredo sauce to cover the bottom of the casserole; sprinkle with a pinch of nutmeg and half the parsley. Layer 3 lasagna noodles and half of each: the cottage cheese, chicken, Parmesan, asparagus, mushrooms, cauliflower, and mozzarella. Spread half the remaining sauce over the mozzarella, sprinkle with another pinch of nutmeg and the remaining parsley. Repeat the layering, ending with noodles, sauce, mozzarella and the remaining Parmesan cheese.

Step 4: BAKE AND SERVE

Bake the lasagna for 45 to 55 minutes, or until golden.

• MAKES 8-10 SERVINGS •

Baked Chicken Ziti

Pasta oozing with melted cheese...the ultimate in comfort food!

	Kosher salt to taste
8	ounces ziti
2	cups diced rotisserie chicken
1	28-ounce jar prepared chunky garden style pasta sauce
1	8-ounce container sour cream
½	cup loosely packed basil leaves, chopped
2	cups shredded Italian blend cheese

Step 1: PREHEAT OVEN AND PREPARE CASSEROLE DISH

Preheat the oven to 350° F. Spray a 2-quart casserole dish with cooking spray.

Step 2: COOK PASTA

Bring a large stockpot three fourths full of water to a boil; lightly season with kosher salt. Stir in the ziti. Cook for 4 to 5 minutes. The pasta should be very undercooked. Drain.

Step 3: MAKE SAUCE

Stir together the chicken, pasta sauce, sour cream and cooked ziti.

Step 4: ASSEMBLE CASSEROLE

Pour half the sauced ziti in the casserole dish; sprinkle with half the basil and half the cheese. Pour in the remaining ziti, followed by the remaining basil and remaining cheese.

Step 5: BAKE

Bake for 10 to 15 minutes or until the ziti is tender but firm and the cheese is melted.

• MAKES 4-6 SERVINGS •

Chicken Tetrazzini

Creamy sauce with just a hint of thyme smothers regular spaghetti in this casserole.

4	tablespoons canola oil
2	tablespoons butter
1	cup frozen diced onions
1	8-ounce package sliced mushrooms
1	teaspoon garlic
¼	cup sherry or white wine
¼	cup all-purpose flour
1	cup chicken broth
2	cups heavy cream
2	cups diced rotisserie chicken
1	teaspoon fresh thyme leaves
	Kosher salt to taste
	Ground black pepper to taste
1	8-ounce package spaghetti, broken into 2 to 3 inch pieces
½	cup grated Parmesan cheese

Step 1: PREHEAT OVEN AND PREPARE CASSEROLE DISH

Preheat the oven to 350° F. Spray a 2-quart casserole dish with cooking spray.

Step 2: SWEAT VEGETABLES

Place the oil and butter in a large saucepan over medium heat; stir in the onions and mushrooms. Cook, stirring frequently, for 4 to 6 minutes or until the onions are translucent. Stir in the garlic and cook 1 minute more. Stir in the sherry to deglaze the pan.

Step 3: MAKE ROUX

Sprinkle the flour over the vegetables. Cook, stirring frequently, for 3 to 4 minutes or until the flour is golden. Slowly stir in the chicken broth. Cook, whisking constantly, for 4 to 6 minutes or until smooth and thick. Stir in the chicken and thyme. Bring to a boil.

Step 4: FINISH SAUCE

Reduce the heat to low. Whisk in the heavy cream; check the seasoning, adding salt and pepper as needed. Stir in the spaghetti and cook, stirring frequently, for 5 minutes.

Step 5: ASSEMBLE AND BAKE

Pour into the prepared casserole; sprinkle with Parmesan. Bake for 12 to 15 minutes or until the pasta is tender but firm and the cheese is golden.

• MAKES 4-6 SERVINGS •

꘍   ꘍   ꘍

Chicken and Potato Casserole

This cheesy casserole has just a hint of heat from the pepper jack cheese.

1	cup diced rotisserie chicken
1/2	cup diced cooked ham
2	cups frozen Southern style (cubed) hash browns
1	cup shredded pepper jack cheese
1	cup shredded Cheddar cheese
1	cup frozen diced onions
2	teaspoons minced garlic
1	16-ounce container sour cream
1	cup heavy cream
1/4	cup chopped loosely packed flat leaf parsley
2	green onions, sliced
	Kosher salt to taste
	Ground black pepper to taste
1	cup seasoned croutons, coarsely crushed

Step 1: PREHEAT OVEN AND PREPARE CASSEROLE DISH

Preheat the oven to 350° F. Spray a 2½-quart casserole dish with cooking spray.

Step 2: ASSEMBLE AND BAKE

Mix together the chicken, ham, hash browns, jack cheese, Cheddar cheese, onion, garlic, sour cream, heavy cream, parsley, green onion, salt, and pepper in a medium bowl. Spread the mixture evenly into the prepared casserole dish. Sprinkle evenly with crouton crumbs. Bake for 30 to 40 minutes or until hot and lightly golden.

• MAKES 8-10 SERVINGS •

Garlicky Chicken and Mushroom Casserole

Rigatoni covered in a creamy chicken and mushroom sauce packed with garlic—vampires beware!

	Kosher salt to taste
8	ounces rigatoni
4	tablespoons olive oil, divided
4	tablespoons butter, divided
1	cup frozen diced onion
1	pound small white button mushrooms, halved
3	teaspoons minced garlic
¼	cup all-purpose flour
4	cup chicken broth
3	cups diced rotisserie chicken
2	cups heavy cream
½	cup loosely packed basil leaves, chopped
1	cup Parmesan cheese
	Ground white pepper to taste
1	cup panko (Japanese bread crumbs)

Step 1: PREHEAT OVEN AND PREPARE CASSEROLE DISH

Preheat the oven to 400° F. Spray a 2-quart casserole dish with cooking spray. Set aside. Fill a large stock pot three fourths full of water and place on high heat. Season with salt.

Step 2: COOK PASTA

When the water in stock pot is at a full boil, stir in the pasta and cook for 6 to 8 minutes or until very al dente. Drain and place in a large bowl; toss with 1 tablespoon of olive oil. Set aside.

Step 3: SWEAT VEGETABLES

Place the remaining olive oil and 3 tablespoons of butter into a large saucepan over medium heat. Add the onion; cook for 3 to 4 minutes or until translucent. Stir in the mushrooms; cook, stirring frequently, for an additional 3 to 4 minutes or until the mushroom are softened. Stir in the garlic and cook 1 minute more.

Step 3: MAKE SAUCE

Sprinkle flour over the vegetables; cook, stirring constantly, for 2 to 3 minutes or until the flour begins to become lightly golden. Carefully pour in the broth. Cook, whisking constantly, for 4 to 6 minutes or until thickened. Stir in the chicken; reduce the heat to low. Simmer for 10 minutes. Stir in the cream, and simmer for 10 minutes more.

Step 4: ADD BASIL AND CHEESE

Stir in the basil and Parmesan. Check the seasoning, adding salt and pepper as needed.

Step 5: ASSEMBLE CASSEROLE.

Mix the mushroom cheese sauce with the cooked pasta. Pour into the prepared casserole, spreading evenly. Place the butter in a medium microwave proof bowl. Heat on high for 20 seconds or until melted. Stir the panko into the butter until evenly coated. Sprinkle the buttered panko evenly over the casserole.

Step 6: BAKE

Bake the casserole for 20 minutes or until golden brown. Allow to rest for 5 minutes; serve.

• MAKES 8-10 SERVINGS •

Tamale Pie

Perfect for when you want the taste of tamales without the hassle of making them from scratch.

2	tablespoon canola oil, divided
1½	cup frozen diced onions, divided
½	cup frozen Southwest style corn (with onions and bell peppers)
2	teaspoons minced garlic, divided
2	cups diced rotisserie chicken
1	15-ounce can diced tomatoes
1	tablespoon chili powder
1	teaspoon ground cumin
1	2.25-ounce can sliced olives, reserving several slices for garnish
½	cup loosely packed cilantro leaves, chopped, divided
1½	cups chicken broth
¾	cup yellow cornmeal
	Cayenne pepper to taste
	Kosher salt to taste
	Ground black pepper to taste
1	cup shredded Mexican style cheese
½	cup sour cream

Step 1: PREHEAT OVEN AND PREPARE PAN

Preheat the oven to 375° F. Spray a 9-inch pie plate with cooking spray.

Step 2: MAKE PIE FILLING

Pour 2 tablespoons of oil in a large saucepan over medium heat; stir in 1 cup of onions, the corn, and 1 teaspoon of garlic. Cook, stirring occasionally, for 3 to 4 minutes or until the onions are translucent. Stir in the chicken, tomatoes, chili powder, cumin, olives, and half of the chopped cilantro. Reduce the heat to low; simmer, stirring occasionally, for 15 minutes.

Step 3: MAKE PIE "SHELL"

Pour the remaining oil in a medium saucepan over medium heat; stir in the remaining onions and garlic. Cook, stirring occasionally, for 3 to 4 minutes or until the onions are translucent. Stir in the chicken broth, cornmeal, and remaining cilantro. Cook, stirring constantly, for 5 to 7 minutes or until thick. Spread the cornmeal mixture onto the bottom and sides of the prepared pie plate.

Step 4: ASSEMBLE AND BAKE

Spread the chicken mixture evenly over the cornmeal crust. Sprinkle with cheese blend. Bake for 20 to 30 minutes or until the cheese is melted and golden.

Step 5: GARNISH AND SERVE

Garnish with a dollop of sour cream and the reserved olive slices, and serve.

COOKS NOTES: To kick up the heat even more, stir diced jalapeños into the chicken mixture.

• MAKES 6-8 SERVINGS •

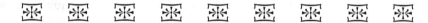

Chicken Amandine Casserole

Almonds provide a tasty crunch in this crowd pleaser!

2	tablespoons canola oil
4	tablespoons butter, divided
1	cup frozen diced onions
2	ribs celery, diced
1	8-ounce package sliced mushrooms
1	cup sliced almonds, divided
3	tablespoons all-purpose flour
3	cups chicken broth
1	cup heavy cream
1	cup uncooked white rice
2	cups diced rotisserie chicken
2	green onions, sliced
1	cup panko (Japanese bread crumbs)

Step 1: SWEAT VEGETABLES

Place the oil and 2 tablespoons of butter in a large skillet over medium heat. Stir in the onions, celery, mushrooms, and almonds. Cook, stirring frequently, for 4 to 6 minutes, or until the onions are translucent. Add the flour; cook, stirring constantly, for 4 to 6 minutes or until lightly golden. Stir in the broth. Cook, whisking constantly, for 8 to 10 minutes or until thick and smooth. Remove from the heat.

Step 2: PREHEAT OVEN AND PREPARE CASSEROLE DISH

Preheat the oven to 400° F. Spray a 2-quart casserole dish with cooking spray. Set aside.

Step 3: ASSEMBLE CASSEROLE

Stir the cream, rice, chicken, and onions into the vegetable mixture. Pour into the prepared casserole. Place the remaining butter in a medium microwave proof bowl. Heat on high for 20 seconds or until melted. Stir the panko into the butter until evenly coated. Sprinkle the buttered panko evenly over the casserole.

Step 4: BAKE

Bake for 30 to 40 minutes, or until the rice is tender and the top is golden. Serve hot.

• MAKES 6-8 SERVINGS •

Quick Chicken Divan

Rich hollandaise sauce drenches chicken and broccoli in this elegant yet easy casserole.

½	cup plus 2 tablespoon butter, divided
2	1.25-ounce packages hollandaise sauce mix
2	cups half and half
2	teaspoons lemon zest
3	cups coarsely shredded rotisserie chicken
1	16-ounce package frozen chopped broccoli
2	cups shredded Gruyere cheese
2	cups panko (Japanese bread crumbs)

Step 1: PREHEAT OVEN AND PREPARE CASSEROLE DISH

Preheat the oven to 400° F. Spray a 2-quart casserole dish with cooking spray. Set aside.

Step 2: MAKE HOLLANDAISE SAUCE

Melt ½ cup of butter in a medium saucepan over medium low heat. Pour in the sauce mix and half and half; whisk constantly until the mixture begins to boil. Reduce the heat to low, and stir in the lemon zest. Simmer, stirring occasionally, for 1 minute or until the sauce thickens. Stir in the chicken.

Step 3: ASSEMBLE CASSEROLE

Arrange the broccoli evenly in the prepared casserole dish. Sprinkle with half the cheese, then spread the chicken mixture evenly over the top, followed by the remaining cheese. Place the remaining butter in a medium microwave proof bowl. Heat on high for 20 seconds or until just melted. Stir the panko into the butter until evenly coated. Sprinkle the buttered panko evenly over the casserole.

Step 4: BAKE

Bake the casserole for 20 minutes or until golden. Serve hot.

COOKS NOTES: Replace the broccoli with asparagus tips for a delicious change.

• MAKES 6-8 SERVINGS •

Green Curry Chicken Casserole

Creamy coconut milk and exotic green curry are perfect partners in this out of the ordinary chicken casserole.

2	13.5-ounce cans coconut milk
3	cups chicken broth
2	tablespoons corn starch
2	teaspoons green curry paste, or more to taste
½	cup loosely packed Thai basil, chopped
½	cup loosely packed cilantro, chopped
2	green onions, sliced thin
1	8-ounce package sliced mushrooms
1	10-ounce package frozen chopped spinach, thawed
2	cups diced rotisserie chicken
2	cups uncooked jasmine rice
	Kosher salt to taste
	Ground white pepper to taste
3	tablespoons butter, melted
1	cup panko (Japanese bread crumbs)
½	cup chopped peanuts

Step 1: PREHEAT OVEN AND PREPARE CASSEROLE DISH

Preheat the oven to 350° F. Spray a 3-quart casserole dish with cooking spray.

Step 2: MAKE CASSEROLE FILLING

Whisk together the coconut milk, chicken broth, cornstarch, and curry paste in a medium bowl until smooth. Stir in the Thai basil, cilantro, onions, mushrooms, spinach, chicken, rice, salt, and pepper.

Step 3: ASSEMBLE AND BAKE

Pour the casserole filling into the prepared casserole dish, spreading evenly. Cover and bake for 20 to 30 minutes, or until the rice is tender.

Step 4: MAKE TOPPING

Stir together the butter, panko, and peanuts in a small bowl. Sprinkle the panko mixture evenly over the casserole. Bake uncovered for 10 to 15 minutes or until golden brown.

• MAKES 8-10 SERVINGS •

Mini Polenta Pie Chicken Casseroles

Warm and hearty, these adorable little casseroles really satisfy.

2	tablespoons olive oil
1	cups frozen diced onion
1/2	cup frozen diced carrots
2	teaspoons minced garlic
2	cups chicken broth
1	14.5-ounce can diced Italian seasoned tomatoes
2	cups diced rotisserie chicken
1	cup frozen Southern style hash browns
1/2	cup loosely packed basil, chopped
	Kosher salt to taste
	Ground black pepper to taste
6	1/2-inch slices from a 16-ounce tube of prepared polenta
1/2	cup grated Parmesan cheese

Step 1: SWEAT VEGETABLES

Place the oil in a medium saucepan over medium heat. Stir in the onion, carrots, and garlic. Cook, stirring often, for 4 to 6 minutes or until the onion is translucent. Stir in the chicken broth, tomatoes, and chicken. Reduce the heat to medium-low; simmer for 15 minutes.

Step 2: PREHEAT OVEN AND PREPARE RAMEKINS

Preheat the oven to 350° F. Spray six 1-cup capacity ramekins with cooking spray. Set aside.

Step 3: ASSEMBLE AND BAKE

Stir the hash browns and basil into the vegetable mixture. Check the seasoning, adding salt and pepper as needed. Divide the mixture evenly between the ramekins. Top with a slice of polenta and a sprinkling of Parmesan cheese. Bake for 15 to 20 minutes or until the cheese is golden. Rest for 10 minutes before serving.

• MAKES 6 SERVINGS •

Green Chile and Chicken Cornbread Bake

Comforting cornbread is kicked up with chicken, green chile, and cheese. Add a tossed salad and dinner's served!

2	tablespoon olive oil
2	tablespoons butter
1	cup frozen diced onion
1	cup southwest style frozen corn mix, thawed
1	teaspoon minced garlic
2	eggs
1	cup milk
1	8.5-ounce package corn bread mix
2	cups diced rotisserie chicken
1	4-ounce can diced green chile peppers
¼	cup loosely packed cilantro leaves, chopped
1	cup Crema Mexicana
½	cup heavy cream
2	cups shredded Monterey Jack cheese, divided

Step 1: PREHEAT OVEN AND PREPARE CASSEROLE DISH

Preheat the oven to 350° F. Spray a 2-quart casserole dish with cooking spray.

Step 2: SWEAT VEGETABLES

Place the olive oil and butter in a large skillet over medium heat; add the onions. Cook, stirring occasionally, for 4 to 5 minutes or until translucent. Stir in the corn mix and garlic; cook for an additional 3 to 4 minutes or until the garlic is just lightly golden. Remove from the heat.

Step 3: MAKE CORNBREAD BATTER

Beat together the eggs and milk in a medium bowl. Stir in the cooled vegetables and corn bread mix. Stir until the batter just comes together, do not overmix.

Step 4: MAKE CASSEROLE FILLING

Mix together the chicken, green chiles (including juice), cilantro, Crema Mexicana, heavy cream, and half of the cheese in a medium bowl.

Step 5: ASSEMBLE CASSEROLE

Pour the batter into prepared casserole dish. Spread the chicken mixture evenly over the corn bread batter. Sprinkle with the remaining cheese. Bake for 30 to 40 minutes or until the cheese is golden.

COOKS NOTES: To kick up the heat a bit, toss in a minced jalapeño along with the diced green chiles.

• MAKES 8-10 SERVINGS •

Tortilla Casserole

Crunchy, creamy and cheesy…who could ask for more?

2	tablespoons canola oil
1	cup frozen diced onion
4	cups frozen bell pepper mix, thawed slightly and diced
2	teaspoons minced garlic
1	tablespoon ground cumin
1	teaspoon cayenne pepper
1	15.5-ounce can black beans, rinsed and drained
1	15-ounce can kidney beans, rinsed and drained
1	10-ounce package frozen corn kernels
3	cups diced rotisserie chicken
1	14.5-ounce can crushed tomatoes
	Kosher salt to taste
	Ground black pepper to taste
8	cups corn tortilla chips
2	cups Crema Mexicana
1	cup loosely packed cilantro, chopped
2	cups shredded Monterey Jack cheese

Step 1: PREHEAT OVEN AND PREPARE CASSEROLE DISH

Preheat the oven to 350° F. Spray a 3-quart casserole dish with cooking spray.

Step 2: SWEAT VEGETABLES

Pour the oil in a large skillet over medium heat; add the onion and bell pepper mix. Cook for 4 to 6 minutes or until the onion is translucent. Stir in the garlic and cook for 1 minute more.

Step 3: COMPLETE FILLING

Stir in the cumin, cayenne, black and kidney beans, corn, chicken, and tomatoes. Bring to a boil. Reduce the heat to low; cook, stirring occasionally, for 15 minutes. Check the seasoning, adding salt and pepper as needed.

Step 4: ASSEMBLE AND BAKE

Cover the bottom of the prepared casserole with half the tortilla chips. Spread half of the chicken mixture over the tortillas, followed by half of the Crema Mexicana, half of the cilantro, and half of the Monterey Jack. Repeat the layers, ending with Monterey Jack cheese. Bake for 30 to 40 minutes or until the cheese is bubbling and lightly golden.

• MAKES 6-8 SERVINGS •

Parmesan Chicken and Eggplant Bake

Prepared marinara and rotisserie chicken get this Italian classic on the table in no time!

5	or 6 small Japanese eggplants
¼	cup olive oil
	Kosher salt to taste
	Ground black pepper to taste
1	48-ounce jar garden style marinara sauce
2	cups grated Parmesan cheese
3	cups shredded rotisserie chicken
½	cup loosely packed basil leaves, chopped
2	cups shredded mozzarella cheese

Step 1: PREHEAT OVEN AND PREPARE CASSEROLE DISH

Preheat the oven to 400° F. Spray a 2-quart casserole dish with cooking spray.

Step 2: ROAST EGGPLANT

Slice the eggplants into ¼-inch rounds. Toss with olive oil in a medium bowl; season with salt and pepper. Arrange the eggplant on a baking sheet. Roast for 20 to 30 minutes, turning half way through cooking, or until lightly browned. Set aside. Reduce the oven temperature to 350°F.

Step 3: ASSEMBLE AND BAKE

Pour half of the marinara sauce into the casserole dish. Tip the dish from side to side to spread the sauce evenly. Arrange the roasted eggplant on the sauce, overlapping as needed to fill the space. Sprinkle half the Parmesan cheese evenly over the eggplant, followed by the chicken, then basil. Top with the mozzarella and remaining Parmesan. Bake for 30 to 40 minutes or until the cheese is melted and becomes golden.

• MAKES 8-10 SERVINGS •

Baked Orzo with Chicken and Spinach

Lemon and thyme enhance the flavor of this creamy casserole.

4	cups chicken broth
1	pound orzo pasta
¼	cup butter, divided
1	cup frozen diced onion
1	8-ounce package sliced mushrooms
½	cup Pinot Gris wine
½	cup heavy cream
2	teaspoons fresh thyme
2	cups diced rotisserie chicken
2	cups loosely packed fresh baby spinach, chopped
1	cup shredded Gruyere cheese
1	cup shredded fontina cheese
	Kosher salt to taste
	Ground white pepper to taste
½	cup dry bread crumbs
¼	cup grated Parmesan cheese
1	teaspoon lemon zest

Step 1: PREHEAT OVEN AND PREPARE CASSEROLE DISH

Preheat the oven to 400° F. Spray a 2-quart casserole dish with cooking spray.

Step 2: COOK ORZO

Bring the chicken broth to a boil in a large saucepan over medium high heat. Stir in the orzo; cook for 7 to 9 minutes or until al dente. Remove from heat; set aside.

Step 3: SWEAT ONIONS AND MUSHROOMS

Melt half the butter in a large skillet over medium heat. Stir in the onion and mushrooms; cook for 4 to 5 minutes or until the onions are translucent. Stir in the wine. Cook, stirring occasionally, for 10 to 15 minutes or until the wine is reduced by half. Reduce the heat to low. Stir in the cream and half the thyme.

Step 4: FINISH CASSEROLE

Stir the mushroom mixture, chicken, spinach, Gruyere, and fontina into the orzo. Check the seasoning, adding salt and pepper as needed.

Step 5: ASSEMBLE AND BAKE

Pour into the prepared casserole dish. Place the remaining butter in a small microwave safe bowl. Microwave on high for 20 to 30 seconds or until just melted. Mix the bread crumbs, Parmesan, lemon zest, and remaining thyme in the butter. Sprinkle evenly over the casserole. Bake for 20 to 30 minutes or until heated through and lightly golden. Rest for 10 minutes before serving.

• MAKES 6-8 SERVINGS •

Chicken and Cheddar Dumplings Casserole

Warm and comforting best describes this dish.

1	tablespoon olive oil
1	tablespoon butter
½	cup frozen diced onions
2	cups frozen Southern style (cubed) hash browns, thawed
2	cups frozen peas and carrots, thawed
2	cups diced rotisserie chicken
2	12-ounce jars home style chicken gravy
1	cup chicken broth
1	teaspoon fresh thyme leaves
1	cup heavy cream
	Kosher salt to taste
	Ground black pepper to taste
2½	cups buttermilk biscuit mix
1	teaspoon minced garlic
1	green onion, sliced thinly
1	cup shredded Cheddar cheese
1	cup milk

Step 1: PREHEAT OVEN AND PREPARE CASSEROLE DISH

Preheat the oven to 400° F. Spray a 2-quart shallow casserole dish with cooking spray; set aside.

Step 2: START CASSEROLE FILLING

Place the olive oil and butter in a large saucepan over medium high heat; add the onions. Cook the onions, stirring occasionally, for 3 to 4 minutes or until translucent. Stir in the hash browns, peas and carrots, chicken, gravy, broth, and thyme. Bring to a boil; cook until heated through. Reduce the heat to low, stir in the heavy cream. Check the seasoning, adding salt and pepper as needed.

Step 3: MAKE DUMPLING TOPPING

Mix together the biscuit mix, garlic, green onion, Cheddar cheese, and milk in a medium bowl. Stir until the dough just comes together, do not overmix.

Step 4: ASSEMBLE CASSEROLE

Pour the casserole filling into the prepared casserole dish. Drop the dumpling mix by heaping tablespoons over the entire surface of the casserole.

Step 5: BAKE

Bake, covered, for 10 minutes. Remove the cover and bake for an additional 15 minutes or until the dumplings are lightly golden.

• MAKES 6-8 SERVINGS •

Chicken Egg Foo Young Casserole

Classic Chinese flavors in the convenience of a scrumptious casserole.

3	tablespoons sesame oil, divided
2	cups frozen Asian mixed vegetables, thawed
1	teaspoon minced garlic
2	cups package angel hair-shredded cabbage
8	large eggs
4	tablespoons soy sauce, divided
	Pinch ground black pepper
1	8-ounce can sliced bamboo shoots-strips, rinsed and drained
2	cups diced rotisserie chicken
1	cup fresh bean sprouts
1	12-ounce jar chicken gravy
2	green onions, sliced thinly on the bias

Step 1: PREHEAT OVEN AND PREPARE CASSEROLE DISH

Preheat the oven to 350° F. Spray a 9x13 casserole dish with cooking spray.

Step 2: SWEAT VEGETABLES

Pour 2 tablespoons of oil into a large skillet over medium high heat; stir in the mixed vegetables and garlic. Cook, stirring occasionally, for 4 to 6 minutes or until crisp-tender. Add the cabbage; cook for an additional 2 to 3 minutes or until just softened. Remove from the heat.

Step 3: MAKE CASSEROLE FILLING

Beat the eggs, 2 tablespoons of soy sauce, and pepper in a large mixing bowl. Stir in the bamboo shoots, chicken, bean sprouts, and cooled vegetable mixture.

Step 4: ASSEMBLE AND BAKE

Pour the mixture into the prepared casserole dish. Bake uncovered for 40 to 50 minutes or until golden.

Step 5: MAKE FOO YOUNG GRAVY

Stir together the gravy, remaining oil, and soy sauce in a microwave safe bowl. Heat on high for 1 to 2 minutes or until hot.

Step 6: GARNISH AND SERVE

Sprinkle the casserole with green onions. Pass hot gravy with the casserole.

• MAKES 8-10 SERVINGS •

Creamy Chicken and Green Bean Casserole

Crisp green beans and creamy chicken sauce create a comforting casserole perfect for a potluck!

2	tablespoons olive oil
1	tablespoons butter
1	cup frozen diced onion
1	8-ounce package sliced mushrooms
¼	cup all-purpose flour
2	cup chicken broth
1	cup diced rotisserie chicken
2	teaspoons fresh thyme leaves
	Ground white pepper to taste
1	teaspoon kosher salt
2	cups uncooked egg noodles
1	12-ounce package frozen whole green and yellow beans, thawed and cut in half
1	cup sour cream
2	cups shredded Monterey Jack cheese
½	cup grated Parmesan cheese

Step 1: PREHEAT OVEN AND PREPARE CASSEROLE DISH

Preheat the oven to 350° F. Spray a 2-quart shallow casserole dish with cooking spray. Set aside.

Step 2: MAKE CREAMY CHICKEN SAUCE

Pour the olive oil in a large saucepan over medium high heat; add the onions and mushrooms. Cook, stirring occasionally, for 3 to 4 minutes or until the onions are translucent. Add the flour; cook, stirring constantly, for 4 to 6 minutes or until lightly golden. Slowly stir in the chicken broth. Cook, whisking constantly, for 8 to 10 minutes or until thick and smooth. Stir in the chicken and thyme. Season with pepper. Bring to a boil, stirring frequently. Reduce the heat to low; simmer for 10 minutes.

Step 3: COOK NOODLES

While the sauce is simmering, bring a large stock pot of water to boil; season with 1 teaspoon of salt. Add the noodles; cook for 4 to 6 minutes or until al dente. Drain; stir into the chicken sauce.

Step 5: ASSEMBLE AND BAKE

Stir the beans, sour cream, and Monterey Jack cheese into the chicken mixture. Pour into the prepared casserole. Sprinkle evenly with the Parmesan cheese. Bake for 20 to 30 minutes or until heated through and the cheese is golden.

COOKS NOTES: For variety, frozen cauliflower or broccoli makes a fine substitution for the green beans.

• MAKES 6-8 SERVINGS •

Lemon-Rosemary Scented Chicken and Potato Gratin

Melted Gruyere between layers of lemony rosemary chicken and potatoes...fabulous!

2	cups diced rotisserie chicken
1	tablespoon lemon juice
	Zest of 1 lemon
1	teaspoon finely minced rosemary
2	teaspoons minced roasted garlic
1	pound potatoes, peeled and thinly sliced
	Kosher salt to taste
	Ground white pepper to taste
2	cups shredded Gruyere cheese
2	tablespoons all-purpose flour
2	cups heavy cream

Step 1: PREHEAT OVEN AND PREPARE CASSEROLE DISH

Preheat the oven to 375°. Spray a shallow 2-quart casserole dish with cooking spray.

Step 2: SEASON CHICKEN

Mix together the chicken, lemon juice and zest, rosemary, and garlic in a medium bowl.

Step 3: ASSEMBLE GRATIN

Arrange half the potatoes on the bottom of the casserole dish; season with salt and pepper. Sprinkle with half the chicken mixture. Toss the shredded cheese with the flour in a small bowl. Sprinkle half of the flour-coated cheese over the chicken. Next, arrange the remaining potatoes over the cheese, and season with salt and pepper. Spread the remaining chicken over the potatoes, followed by the remaining cheese. Pour the cream over the casserole.

Step 4: BAKE AND SERVE

Bake, covered, for 20 minutes. Remove the cover and bake for an additional 15 to 20 minutes or until the potatoes are tender and the cheese is lightly golden. Let rest for 10 minutes before serving. Garnish with a sprig of rosemary.

• MAKES 6-8 SERVINGS •

Ratatouille Poulet

This humble peasant dish is deliciously updated for today's hectic lifestyle.

3	tablespoons olive oil
2	cups frozen diced onion
1	eggplant, cubed
2	zucchini, sliced
3	teaspoons minced garlic
2	14.5-ounce cans diced tomatoes seasoned with basil and oregano
3	cups coarsely shredded rotisserie chicken
1	cup loosely packed basil, chopped
	Kosher salt to taste
	Ground black pepper to taste
1	cup shredded mozzarella cheese
¼	cup grated Parmesan cheese

Step 1: PREHEAT OVEN AND PREPARE CASSEROLE DISH

Preheat the oven to 350° F. Spray a 2-quart casserole dish with cooking spray.

Step 2: SWEAT VEGETABLES

Pour the oil in a large saucepan over medium heat; stir in the onions, eggplant, and zucchini. Cook, stirring frequently, for 4 to 6 minutes or until softened. Stir in the garlic and cook 1 minute more.

Step 3: ADD TOMATOES AND CHICKEN

Stir in the tomatoes, chicken, and basil; bring to a boil. Check the seasoning, adding salt and pepper as needed.

Step 4: ASSEMBLE CASSEROLE

Pour the chicken mixture into the prepared casserole dish; sprinkle with mozzarella and Parmesan cheese. Bake for 15 to 20 minutes or until the cheese is lightly golden.

COOKS NOTES: Serve in bowls with crusty French bread to sop up all the delicious juice.

• MAKES 4-6 SERVINGS •

Baked Teriyaki Chicken Rigatoni

Just a touch of teriyaki sauce gives such depth to this rich and creamy casserole.

	Kosher salt to taste
8	ounces rigatoni
¼	cup canola oil
2	tablespoons butter
1	cup frozen diced onions
1	teaspoon minced garlic
¼	cup all-purpose flour
1	cup chicken broth
1	cup whole milk
2	cups heavy whipping cream
2	tablespoons prepared teriyaki sauce
2	cups shredded rotisserie chicken
2	green onions, cut in 1-inch pieces on the bias
½	cup sliced almonds

Step 1: PREHEAT OVEN AND PREPARE CASSEROLE DISH

Preheat the oven to 350° F. Spray a 2-quart casserole dish with cooking spray.

Step 2: COOK PASTA

Bring a large stockpot three fourths full of water to a boil; lightly season with kosher salt. Stir in the rigatoni. Cook for 4 to 5 minutes. The pasta should be very undercooked. Drain.

Step 3: SWEAT VEGETABLES

Place the oil and butter in a large saucepan over medium heat; stir in the onions. Cook, stirring frequently, for 3 to 4 minutes or until the onions are translucent. Stir in the garlic; cook for 1 minute more.

Step 4: MAKE ROUX

Sprinkle the flour over the onions; cook, whisking constantly, for 2 to 3 minutes or until the flour is golden. Slowly whisk in the broth; cook, whisking constantly, for 4 to 6 minutes or until thickened. Reduce the heat to low.

Step 5: FINISH SAUCE

Stir in the milk, whipping cream, teriyaki sauce, chicken, green onions, and cooked pasta.

Step 6: BAKE

Pour the sauced rigatoni into the prepared casserole. Bake, covered, for 15 minutes. Sprinkle with almonds and continue baking, uncovered, for 10 to 15 minutes or until the rigatoni is tender, but firm.

• MAKES 4-6 SERVINGS •

Chicken and Fig Casserole

Figs add unexpected and delicious sweetness to this casserole.

1	pound challah bread, cut into 1 inch cubes
4	slices bacon, diced
1	cup frozen diced onion
1	8-ounce package sliced mushrooms
1	teaspoon minced garlic
½	cup Pinot Gris or other white wine
1	tablespoons fresh thyme
4	eggs
2	cups milk
	Kosher salt to taste
	Ground black pepper to taste
2	cups rotisserie chicken, diced
6	fresh figs, diced
2	cups shredded Monterey Jack cheese

Step 1: PREHEAT OVEN AND PREPARE CASSEROLE DISH

Preheat the oven to 350° F. Spray a 2-quart casserole dish with cooking spray.

Step 2: TOAST CHALLAH

Spread the bread cubes on an ungreased baking sheet. Bake for 15 to 20 minutes or until lightly toasted. Cool.

Step 3: COOK BACON AND SWEAT VEGETABLES

Place the bacon in a large skillet over medium heat. Cook, stirring frequently, for 3 to 4 minutes or until crisp. Remove the bacon to a plate; set aside. Stir in the onion and mushrooms. Cook, stirring frequently, for 4 to 6 minutes or until the onions are translucent. Stir in the garlic and cook for 1 minute more. Pour in the wine to deglaze the skillet; stir in the thyme. Remove from the heat.

Step 4: ASSEMBLE CASSEROLE

Place the bread cubes in the prepared casserole. Beat together the eggs and milk, season to taste with salt and pepper; pour over the bread cubes. Sprinkle evenly with the chicken and figs. Spread the mushroom mixture over the top; sprinkle with cheese. Cover and refrigerate for 30 minutes.

Step 5: BAKE AND SERVE

Bake, covered, for 30 minutes; uncover and continue baking for an additional 15 to 20 minutes or until lightly golden.

• MAKES 6-8 SERVINGS •

Chicken Enchilada Suiza Casserole

This casserole has all the great flavor of enchilada suizas without the long preparation.

1	16-ounce jar salsa verde (medium or hot)
1	pint plus 1 cup Crema Mexicana, divided
18	6-inch corn tortillas, cut into fourths
1	cup frozen diced onion
4	cups baby spinach leaves, torn into bite size pieces
1	cup loosely packed cilantro leaves, chopped
2	cups shredded rotisserie chicken
1	8-ounce packages sliced mushrooms
2	cups shredded Monterey Jack cheese
1	green onion, sliced

Step 1: PREHEAT OVEN AND PREPARE CASSEROLE DISH

Preheat the oven to 350° F. Spray a 3-quart inch casserole with cooking spray.

Step 2: MAKE SAUCE

Mix together the salsa verde and 1 pint of Crema Mexicana in a bowl you can easily pour from (a large measuring pitcher works well). Set aside.

Step 3: ASSEMBLE CASSEROLE

Pour enough sauce to just cover the bottom into the casserole dish. Next, layer one third of the ingredients evenly in the following order: tortillas, onion, spinach, cilantro, chicken, mushrooms, sauce, and cheese. Repeat with 2 more layers, ending with cheese.

Step 4: BAKE AND SERVE

Cover and bake for 30 to 40 minutes. Remove the cover and bake for 15 to 20 minutes more, or until the cheese is lightly golden. Allow to rest for 10 minutes. Garnish with the remaining Crema Mexicana and green onion.

COOKS NOTES: Crema Mexicana can be found in many well-stocked grocery stores or in Mexican markets. It is similar to sour cream or crème fraiche. You may substitute either.

• MAKES 8-10 SERVINGS •

BREAKFASTS AND BRUNCHES

Chicken and Asparagus Crêpes

Crepes are a natural at the brunch table; store bought ones simplify this recipe.

1	tablespoon minced flat leaf parsley
2	1.25-ounce packages hollandaise sauce mix, prepared according to package instructions
1	tablespoon butter
1	shallot, minced
2½	cups diced rotisserie chicken
½	cup bacon pieces
	Pinch ground nutmeg
30	asparagus spears, blanched
10	prepared crêpes
1	cup grated fontina cheese
¼	cup milk

Step 1: PREHEAT OVEN AND PREPARE PAN

Preheat the oven to 350° F. Spray a 9x13 baking pan with cooking spray.

Step 2: MAKE SAUCE

Mix the parsley into the prepared hollandaise sauce; set aside.

Step 3: MAKE FILLING

Melt the butter in a large skillet over medium heat; add the shallot. Cook, stirring occasionally, for 3 to 4 minutes or until translucent. Stir in the chicken, bacon, half the prepared hollandaise sauce, and nutmeg.

Step 4: ASSEMBLE CREPES

Pat dry the asparagus with paper towels; arrange 3 asparagus spears in the center of a crêpe. Place ¼ cup of chicken mixture over the asparagus; sprinkle with a tablespoonful of cheese. Roll the crêpe, and place seam side down in the prepared baking pan. Continue to assemble crêpes with the remaining ingredients.

Step 5: SAUCE AND BAKE

Mix the milk into the remaining hollandaise sauce; pour over the crêpes. Bake for 20 minutes or until hot and bubbly.

COOKS NOTES: Blanched cauliflower or broccoli florettes make a nice substitution for the asparagus.

• MAKES 4-6 SERVINGS •

Creamy Chicken Tarragon Crêpes

Hollandaise sauce mix and rotisserie chicken get this luxurious brunch on the table quickly!

2	1.25-ounce packages hollandaise sauce mix, prepared according to package directions
1	tablespoons finely chopped tarragon, plus more for garnish
2½	cups diced rotisserie chicken
10	prepared crêpes
¼	cup milk

Step 1: PREHEAT OVEN AND PREPARE PAN

Preheat the oven to 350° F. Spray a 9x13 inch baking pan with cooking spray.

Step 2: MAKE FILLING

Mix together half the prepared hollandaise sauce and all of the tarragon and chicken in a small bowl.

Step 3: ASSEMBLE CREPES

Place ¼ cup of chicken mixture down the center of a crêpe. Roll the crêpe, and place seam side down in the prepared baking pan. Continue to assemble crêpes with the remaining ingredients.

Step 4: SAUCE AND BAKE

Mix the milk into the remaining hollandaise sauce; pour over the crêpes. Bake for 20 minutes or until hot and bubbly.

COOKS NOTES: Many well-stocked markets carry prepared crêpes in their produce section.

• MAKES 4-6 SERVINGS •

Asparagus and Chicken Eggs Benedict

Rich and decadent, and oh so delicious.

2	English muffins
1	teaspoon white vinegar
4	large eggs
8	to 10 asparagus spears, trimmed to fit atop muffin, blanched (see Cooks Note, below)
1	breast cut from a rotisserie chicken, thinly sliced
1	1.25-ounce package hollandaise sauce mix, prepared according to package instructions
1	tablespoon chopped chives

Step 1: TOAST MUFFINS

Split the English muffins and toast to the desired doneness.

Step 2: POACH EGGS

Fill a small skillet with 2 inches of water. Bring to a gentle boil over medium high heat. Add the vinegar to the water. Crack each egg into a cup. Gently slide the eggs into the water. Cook until the whites are opaque and the yolks are still soft, about $2\frac{1}{2}$ to 3 minutes. Gently remove the eggs with a slotted spoon to a warm plate.

Step 3: ASSEMBLE & SERVE

Place the muffins cut side up on a plate; top each with asparagus, then an equal portion of chicken. Place an egg on top of the chicken; ladle 3 to 4 tablespoons of hollandaise sauce over the egg. Garnish with chives and serve.

COOKS NOTES: To blanch the asparagus, bring a large skillet halfway full of water to a boil. Season with salt. Sprinkle a teaspoon of baking soda in the boiling water. Place all of the asparagus in the water; return to a boil. Immediately remove the asparagus to a bowl of cool water to stop the cooking.

• MAKES 2 SERVINGS •

Chicken Caprese Strata

Fresh tomatoes, basil and garlic come together deliciously in this brunch favorite.

½	pound Italian bread, cut into ½-inch cubes
1	cup milk
1	teaspoon minced garlic
1	teaspoon lemon zest
4	to 5 Roma tomatoes, sliced
½	cup loosely packed basil leaves, chopped
2	cups shredded rotisserie chicken
2	cups shredded mozzarella cheese
4	large eggs
½	cup whole milk
1	teaspoon Kosher salt
½	teaspoon ground black pepper

Step 1: PREPARE CASSEROLE DISH

Spray a 2-quart casserole dish with cooking spray.

Step 2: MAKE FIRST LAYER

Cover the bottom of the prepared casserole dish with the bread cubes. Mix the milk, garlic, and lemon zest in a small bowl; pour over the bread. Set aside until the bread absorbs most of the milk.

Step 3: ASSEMBLE STRATA

Arrange the tomato slices in a single layer over the bread cubes; sprinkle with the basil. Layer the chicken, followed by the cheese. Beat together the eggs, milk, salt, and pepper in a medium bowl; pour over the strata. Cover and refrigerate for 6 to 8 hours.

Step 4: BAKE AND SERVE

Preheat the oven to 350° F. Bake for 45 to 55 minutes or until golden brown.

COOKS NOTES: We particularly enjoy this served with links of sweet Italian sausage.

• MAKES 6-8 SERVINGS •

Crustless Chicken Broccoli-Cheddar Quiche

Served with a garden or fruit salad, this makes a wonderful light meal.

1	tablespoon olive oil
1	tablespoon butter
½	cup diced frozen onions
2	teaspoons minced garlic
5	eggs, beaten
1	cup heavy cream
1	cup cottage cheese
½	teaspoon nutmeg
½	teaspoon ground white pepper
½	16-ounce package chopped broccoli, thawed
2	cups diced rotisserie chicken
2	cups shredded white Cheddar cheese

Step 1: PREHEAT OVEN AND PREPARE BAKING DISH

Preheat the oven to 350° F. Spray a 9-inch pie plate with cooking spray.

Step 2: SWEAT ONIONS

Place the oil and butter in a medium skillet over medium high heat; stir in the onions and garlic. Cook, stirring occasionally, for 2 to 3 minutes or until the onion is translucent. Set aside.

Step 3: ASSEMBLE QUICHE

Beat together the eggs, cream, cottage cheese, nutmeg, and pepper in a large bowl. Stir in the broccoli, chicken, and Cheddar cheese.

Step 4: BAKE AND SERVE

Pour the mixture into the prepared baking dish. Bake for 45 to 55 minutes, or until the eggs are set and the top is golden. Serve hot.

• MAKES 6-8 SERVINGS •

Mini Jalapeño Chicken Quiches

Adorable bite sized quiches, perfect for Sunday brunch.

2	9-inch refrigerator pie crusts, brought to room temperature according to package instructions
1	slice bacon, diced
1	small jalapeño, seeded and minced
1	teaspoon minced garlic
4	large eggs
1/4	cup milk
1/2	cup finely diced rotisserie chicken
1	green onion, sliced
3/4	cup shredded Mexican cheese blend
1/4	cup loosely packed cilantro, chopped

Step 1: PREHEAT OVEN AND PREPARE QUICHE CRUSTS

Preheat the oven to 425° F. Using a 3-inch round cookie cutter, cut 8 circles out of each pie crust. Line muffin pan cups with a pastry round.

Step 2: START FILLING

Place the bacon in a heavy skillet over medium heat. Cook, stirring occasionally, for 4 to 6 minutes or until crisp. Remove the bacon with a slotted spoon; drain on a paper towel-lined plate. Stir the jalapeño into the bacon drippings; cook, stirring occasionally, for 3 to 4 minutes or until soft. Add the garlic and cook 1 minute more. Remove from the heat.

Step 3: COMPLETE FILLING

Beat together the eggs and milk in a medium bowl. Stir in the chicken, green onion, cooked bacon, jalapeño, and cheese.

Step 4: ASSEMBLE AND BAKE

Divide the filling evenly between the pastry shells. Bake for 15 to 20 minutes or until firm and golden. Sprinkle with cilantro and serve.

• MAKES 8-10 SERVINGS •

Chicken Florentine Quiche

Spinach and creamy Gruyere are perfect partners in this quiche.

½	pound mushrooms
3	tablespoons butter
½	cup panko (Japanese bread crumbs)
¼	grated Parmesan cheese
1	teaspoon fresh thyme
2	cups shredded Gruyere cheese
3	tablespoons all-purpose flour
1	10-ounce package frozen chopped spinach, thawed and drained
2	cups diced rotisserie chicken
4	eggs, beaten
1	cup heavy cream
2	green onions, sliced
1	teaspoon minced garlic
1	teaspoon lemon zest
	Kosher salt to taste
	Ground white pepper to taste

Step 1: PREHEAT OVEN AND PREPARE PAN

Preheat the oven to 350°F. Spray a 9-inch deep dish pie pan with cooking spray.

Step 2: MAKE CRUST

Place the mushrooms in the bowl of a food processor fit with a metal blade; pulse in 3-second bursts until coarsely minced. Melt the butter in a medium skillet over medium heat; stir in the mushrooms. Cook, stirring occasionally, for 4 to 6 minutes or until they begin to turn golden and release their liquid. Remove from the heat. Stir in the panko, Parmesan cheese, and thyme. Press the mixture into the bottom and up the sides of the prepared pie pan to form the crust. Set aside.

Step 3: MAKE FILLING

Toss the Gruyere cheese and flour in a medium bowl. Mix in the spinach, chicken, eggs, cream, onion, garlic, lemon zest, salt, and pepper. Pour the mixture into the crust; spread evenly.

Step 4: BAKE AND SERVE

Bake the quiche for 35 to 45 minutes or until set and lightly golden. Rest for 10 minutes. Cut into wedges and serve.

• MAKES 6-8 SERVINGS •

☒   ☒   ☒

Steamed Egg Cups with Chicken and Enoki

This decidedly elegant way to serve eggs is much simpler to make than you'd expect.

4	large eggs
2	cups chicken broth
2	teaspoons white wine
1	teaspoon low sodium soy sauce
1/2	cup finely chopped rotisserie chicken white meat
	Pinch ground white pepper
20	enoki mushrooms, washed and trimmed
1	teaspoon chives, chopped plus more for garnish

Step 1: PREHEAT OVEN AND PREPARE RAMEKINS

Preheat the oven to 350° F. Spray four 1-cup ramekins with cooking spray.

Step 2: MAKE EGG CUPS

Beat the eggs, broth, wine, soy sauce, chicken, and pepper in a medium bowl. Place 5 mushrooms and a sprinkling of chives into each ramekin. Pour the egg mixture evenly into the 4 ramekins.

Step 3: COOK EGG CUPS

Place the ramekins into a baking pan. Fill the pan halfway the distance of the ramekin height with hot water. Bake for 30 to 40 minutes, or until the eggs are set with the consistency of silken tofu. Sprinkle with additional chives and serve.

• MAKES 4-6 SERVINGS •

Chicken and Wild Mushroom Crustless Quiche

Earthy mushrooms paired perfectly with fontina and thyme for a scrumptious breakfast or brunch.

1	teaspoon butter
1	teaspoon olive oil
1	cup frozen diced onions
1	pound various mushrooms (morel, crimini, trumpet, button, etc.), cut into bite-sized pieces
1	teaspoon minced garlic
½	cup cooked bacon pieces
1	teaspoon fresh thyme
¼	cup white wine
5	eggs, beaten
1	cup milk
1	cup cottage cheese
2	cups rotisserie chicken
1	cup shredded provolone cheese
1	cup shredded fontina cheese

Step 1: PREHEAT OVEN AND PREPARE PAN

Preheat the oven to 350 ° F. Spray a 9-inch pie pan or small casserole with cooking spray. Set aside.

Step 2: SWEAT VEGETABLES

Heat the butter and olive oil in a large skillet over medium heat; Stir in the onions. Cook, stirring frequently, for 3 to 4 minutes or until translucent. Stir in the mushrooms; cook, stirring frequently, for 4 to 6 minutes or until the mushrooms just begin to brown. Stir in the garlic, bacon, and thyme; cook 1 minute more. Deglaze the skillet with the wine, taking care to scrape the brown bits from the bottom of the skillet. Remove from the heat. Set aside.

Step 3: COMBINE QUICHE FILLING

Beat together the eggs and milk in a medium bowl. Stir in the cottage cheese, chicken, provolone and fontina cheeses, and mushroom mixture.

Step 4: BAKE

Pour the filling into the prepared pie pan. Bake for 35 to 40 minutes or until the eggs are set and the top is golden.

COOKS NOTE: To make this quiche even more special, bake in small ramekins; just reduce the cooking time to about 20 minutes.

• MAKES 6-8 SERVINGS •

Chicken Quiche Mediterranean

Classic Mediterranean ingredients pack this quiche with rich flavor.

1	9-inch purchased refrigerator pie crust
6	eggs, beaten
½	cup ricotta cheese
½	cup mascarpone cheese, softened
2	cups shredded mozzarella cheese
½	cup Asiago cheese
1	cup diced rotisserie chicken
1	cup diced roasted bell peppers
1	6.5-ounce jar marinated quartered artichoke hearts, including marinade
1	2.25-ounce can sliced olives

Step 1: PREHEAT OVEN

Preheat the oven to 350° F.

Step 2: ASSEMBLE PIE CRUST

Line a 9-inch pie plate with pie crust according to the package instructions. Set aside.

Step 3: MAKE FILLING

Mix together the eggs, ricotta, mascarpone, mozzarella, Asiago, chicken, bell peppers, artichoke hearts, and olives in a medium bowl.

Step 4: ASSEMBLE AND BAKE

Pour the filling into the prepared pie crust. Bake for 50 to 60 minutes or until set and golden.

• MAKES 8-10 SERVINGS •

Breakfast Turnovers

Light and flaky puff pastry crust with a savory filling—a wonderful way to start the day!

1	tablespoon canola oil
1	cup frozen Southern style hash brown potatoes
1/2	cup frozen bell pepper and onion mix
1/2	cup diced rotisserie chicken
1	teaspoon fresh thyme
2	eggs, divided
	Kosher salt to taste
	Ground black pepper to taste
1	sheet puff pastry, thawed

Step 1: PREHEAT OVEN AND PREPARE BAKING SHEET

Preheat the oven to 400° F. Spray a baking sheet with cooking spray. Set aside.

Step 2: MAKE TURNOVER FILLING

Pour the oil in a large skillet over medium heat; add hash browns. Cook, without stirring for 7 to 8 minutes or until brown and crisp. Turn the hash browns over and cook for an additional 4 to 5 minutes or until brown. Stir in the bell pepper and onion mix; cook, stirring occasionally, for 3 to 4 minutes or until just softened. Stir in the chicken, thyme, and 1 egg. Cook, stirring frequently, for 3 to 4 minutes or until the egg is just set. Check the seasoning, adding salt and pepper as needed.

Step 3: ASSEMBLE TURNOVERS

On a slightly floured work surface, roll the sheet of puff pastry out into 12x8-inch rectangle. Cut the pastry in half lengthwise then into thirds crosswise, forming 6 squares. Divide the filling evenly among the 6 squares, leaving a 1-inch border all around. Brush the border with beaten egg; fold each square into half, forming a triangle and covering the filling. Crimp the edges with a fork to form a seal.

Step 4: BAKE AND SERVE

Place the turnovers onto the prepared baking sheet. Bake for 10 to 12 minutes or until golden brown.

• MAKES 6 SERVINGS •

Breakfast Burritos

Convenient to eat; perfect for breakfast on the run!

2	tablespoons canola oil
2	tablespoons butter
1	cup diced frozen onions
2	teaspoons minced garlic
2	cups frozen Southern style hash browns, thawed
1	teaspoon ground cumin
2	cups shredded rotisserie chicken
4	large eggs, beaten
¼	cup loosely packed cilantro, chopped
	Kosher salt to taste
	Ground black pepper to taste
4	burrito size flour tortillas, warmed
1	cup shredded pepper jack cheese
	Prepared salsa, to taste
	Sour cream, to taste

Step 1: START BURRITO FILLING

Place the oil and butter in a large skillet over medium heat; stir in the onions, garlic, hash browns, cumin, and chicken. Cook, without stirring for 6 to 8 minutes or until crisp and brown on the bottom. Stir; continue to cook without stirring for another 4 to 6 minutes or until the hash browns are mostly browned.

Step 2: COOK EGGS

Push the hash brown mixture to one side of the skillet to make room for the eggs. Drizzle with a little more oil. Pour the eggs into the skillet. Cook, stirring occasionally, for 2 to 3 minutes, or until the eggs are just set but not dry. Stir the eggs and cilantro into the hash brown mixture. Check the seasoning, adding salt and pepper as needed.

Step 3: ASSEMBLE BURRITOS

Place one fourth of the hash brown mixture in the center of a warmed tortilla. Sprinkle with ¼ cup of cheese and roll up, burrito style. Continue assembling with the remaining ingredients.

Step 4: GARNISH AND SERVE

Place the burritos on serving plates. Garnish as desired with salsa and sour cream. Serve hot.

COOKS NOTES: Increase the heat factor in these by stirring in a bit of minced jalapeño.

• MAKES 4 SERVINGS •

Tarragon Chicken Omelet with Havarti

The creamy filling in this omelet is unexpected and wonderful!

¼	cup diced rotisserie chicken
½	cup shredded Havarti, divided
½	teaspoon minced garlic
1	teaspoon minced fresh tarragon
¼	cup sour cream
3	large eggs, beaten
⅛	cup whole milk
	Pinch garlic powder
	Pinch ground sweet paprika
	Kosher salt
	Ground black pepper

Step 1: MAKE OMELET FILLING

Mix together the chicken, ¼ cup of Havarti, garlic, tarragon, and sour cream in a small mixing bowl. Set aside.

Step 2: MAKE OMELET

Beat together the eggs, milk, garlic powder, paprika, salt, and pepper in a small bowl.

Step 3: COOK OMELET

Spray a small non-stick skillet with cooking spray; place over medium heat. Pour the egg mixture in the pan. Cook, lifting the edges of the eggs as they set and allow the uncooked eggs to flow under the cooked portion. When almost completely set, place the filling on half of the omelet. Slide the omelet out of the pan onto the serving plate; fold in half as it comes out. Sprinkle with the remaining cheese; place under a broiler to melt the cheese. Serve hot.

COOKS NOTES: This omelet pairs perfectly with roasted new potatoes seasoned with rosemary and garlic.

• MAKES 1 SERVING

Chicken and Grits Casserole

Creamy and satisfying with just a touch of heat thanks to pepper jack cheese.

2	cups milk
3	eggs
1	cup diced rotisserie chicken
1	cup frozen diced onion
1	teaspoon minced garlic
1	green onion, sliced
1	cup shredded pepper jack cheese
1	8.5-ounce package corn bread mix
3	tablespoons quick grits
	Kosher salt to taste
	Ground black pepper to taste

Step 1: PREHEAT OVEN AND PREPARE PAN

Preheat the oven to 350° F. Spray a 2-quart casserole dish with cooking spray.

Step 2: MAKE CASSEROLE

Beat together the milk and eggs in a large bowl. Stir in the chicken, diced onion, garlic, green onion, pepper jack cheese, corn bread mix, grits, and salt and pepper.

Step 3: ASSEMBLE AND BAKE

Pour the casserole mixture into the prepared casserole dish. Bake for 45 to 55 minutes, or until set and golden.

COOKS NOTES: To cut back on the heat, substitute some or all of the pepper jack cheese with Cheddar or regular jack cheese.

• MAKES 6-8 SERVINGS •

Chicken Artichoke Frittata

This Italian take on an omelet packed with chicken, potatoes and cheese is a terrific and delicious way to serve a crowd.

2	tablespoon butter
2	tablespoons olive oil
1	cup frozen diced onion
½	8-ounce package sliced mushrooms
1	teaspoons minced garlic
6	eggs
1	cup milk
4	cups frozen Southern style hash browns, thawed
2	cups diced rotisserie chicken
1	6.5-ounce jar marinated artichoke hearts, drained and chopped
1	4-ounce jar diced pimientos, drained
2	cups shredded Italian blend cheese

Step 1: PREHEAT OVEN

Preheat the oven to 400° F.

Step 2: START ONIONS AND MUSHROOMS

Place the butter and oil in a large oven safe skillet over medium high heat. Stir in the onions; cook for 4 to 6 minutes, stirring occasionally, or until translucent. Add the mushrooms; cook for 4 to 6 minutes or until the mushrooms are softened. Stir in the garlic and cook 1 minute more.

Step 3: COMBINE EGG MIXTURE

Beat together the eggs and milk in a large bowl. Stir in the hash browns, chicken, artichokes, pimientos, and cheese.

Step 4: ASSEMBLE AND BAKE

Stir the egg mixture into the skillet with the onions and mushrooms; cook for 15 minutes. Place in the preheated oven; cook for 15 more minutes, or until the eggs are set and the top is golden.

• MAKES 6-8 SERVINGS •

Huevos Rancheros con Pollo

The addition of chicken in this Mexican favorite makes for an even more hearty breakfast.

	Canola oil for cooking
4	small corn tortillas
4	large eggs
1	cup refried beans, warmed
1	cup diced rotisserie chicken, warmed
1	cup shredded Monterey Jack cheese
1	avocado, sliced
1	cup prepared salsa
¼	cup loosely packed cilantro, chopped

Step 1: COOK TORTILLAS

Drizzle 1 tablespoon of canola oil in a large skillet over medium heat. Place a tortilla in skillet, and cook for 2 to 3 minutes, turning half way through, or until golden and crisp. Drain on a paper towel-lined plate. Continue cooking remaining tortillas, adding more oil as needed.

Step 2: FRY EGGS

Pour 2 tablespoons of oil into the skillet over medium high heat. Break the eggs into skillet, cover, and cook for 1 to 2 minutes, or until the whites are set.

Step 3: ASSEMBLE AND SERVE

Spread ¼ cup of refried beans onto each tortilla. Sprinkle each tortilla with ¼ cup of chicken and ¼ cup of cheese. Place on a serving plate. Place a fried egg onto the covered tortilla. Arrange one fourth of the avocado slices over the egg and drizzle ¼ cup of salsa on top. Sprinkle with cilantro. Continue assembling with the remaining ingredients. Serve while hot.

COOKS NOTES: A cool fruit salad with mango makes a fresh accompaniment for this meal.

• MAKES 4 SERVINGS •

Enchilada Stuffed Hash Browns

Chicken enchiladas never had it so good...what a wonderful surprise tucked inside these hash browns!

2	cups diced rotisserie chicken
2	cups shredded Monterey Jack cheese
1	cup frozen diced onion
1	4-ounce can diced green chiles
1	3.8-ounce can sliced olives, reserve several slices for garnish
1/2	cup prepared red enchilada sauce
1	16-ounce container sour cream, reserve 1/4 cup for garnish
2	green onions, sliced
1/2	cup loosely packed cilantro, chopped
1	2-pound package frozen shredded hash brown potatoes, thawed
3	tablespoons butter, melted
	Kosher salt to taste

Step 1: PREHEAT OVEN AND PREPARE PAN

Preheat the oven to 350° F. Spray a 9x13 inch casserole dish with cooking spray.

Step 2: MAKE FILLING

Mix together the chicken, shredded cheeses, diced onion, green chiles, olives, enchilada sauce, sour cream, green onions, and cilantro in a medium bowl. Set aside.

Step 3: ASSEMBLE CASSEROLE

Arrange half the hash browns in the casserole dish, press with the back of a spoon to compact lighly. Pour the filling on top and spread evenly. Arrange the remaining hash browns on top, again pressing with the back of a spoon to compact lightly. Brush the top with melted butter.

Step 4: BAKE AND SERVE

Bake for 30 to 40 minutes or until the potatoes are crisp and golden. Sprinkle with salt. Garnish with the reserved sour cream and olives; serve.

• MAKES 8-10 SERVINGS •

Chicken and Pepper Jack Hash Brown Bake

Southwestern flavors kick up plain hash browns in this casserole.

2	eggs, beaten
1	cup chicken broth
1	8-ounce package cream cheese, softened
1	16-ounce container sour cream
2	teaspoons minced garlic
1	4-ounce can diced green chiles (including juice)
2	cups shredded pepper jack cheese
6	cups frozen Southern-style hash brown potatoes, thawed
1	cup frozen diced onion, thawed
2	cups diced rotisserie chicken
¼	cup loosely packed cilantro, chopped
2	green onions, thinly sliced
	Kosher salt to taste
	Ground black pepper to taste
1	cup panko (Japanese bread crumbs)
2	tablespoons butter, melted

Step 1: PREHEAT OVEN AND PREPARE CASSEROLE DISH

Preheat the oven to 350° F. Spray a 2-quart casserole dish with cooking spray.

Step 2: MIX CASSEROLE

Mix together the eggs, broth, cream cheese, sour cream, garlic, green chiles, jack cheese, potatoes, diced onion, chicken, cilantro, green onion, salt, and pepper. Pour into the prepared casserole dish.

Step 3: FINISH AND BAKE

Stir together the panko and butter in a small bowl. Sprinkle evenly over the casserole. Bake for 45 to 55 minutes or until golden brown.

• MAKES 8-10 SERVINGS •

Waffles and Chicken Gravy

With roots in Pennsylvania Dutch cooking, these make a terrific and filling meal any time of day!

1	tablespoon butter
1	tablespoon canola oil
½	cup frozen diced onion
1	rib celery, diced
½	cup shredded carrot
2	tablespoons all-purpose flour
2	cups chicken broth
2	cups diced rotisserie chicken
1	bay leaf
1	cup heavy cream
	Kosher salt to taste
	Ground white pepper to taste
8	frozen whole grain waffles, toasted

Step 1: SWEAT VEGETABLES

Place the butter and canola oil in a large saucepan over medium high heat; stir in the onion, celery, and carrot. Cook, stirring occasionally, for 4 to 6 minutes or until the onions are translucent.

Step 2: MAKE THE GRAVY

Stir in the flour; cook for 2 to 3 minutes or until the flour is golden. Whisk in the chicken broth; cook, whisking constantly, until the gravy is thick and smooth. Stir in the chicken and bay leaf. Reduce the heat to low; simmer for 10 minutes, stirring occasionally. Stir in the heavy cream; simmer for 10 more minutes. Check the seasoning, adding salt and pepper as needed. Discard the bay leaf.

Step 3: ASSEMBLE AND SERVE

Place 2 waffles staggered on a serving plate; ladle a generous amount of chicken gravy on top. Continue assembling with the remaining ingredients. Serve hot.

COOKS NOTES: This gravy is equally delicious served on toasted bread or buttermilk biscuits.

• MAKES 4 SERVINGS •

Pimento-Chicken Bagel Breakfast Sandwiches

Delightful little sandwiches and so easy to put together.

4	mini plain bagels, split and toasted
1	5-ounce jar pimiento cheese spread
¼	cup whole milk, divided
3	eggs
1	cup shredded rotisserie chicken
1	green onion, sliced, divided
1	tablespoon butter

Step 1: DRESS BAGELS

Spread the cut sides of each bagel with pimiento cheese spread. Set aside.

Step 2: MAKE CHEESE SAUCE

Mix together the remaining pimiento cheese spread and 2 tablespoons of milk in a small microwave proof bowl. Heat in the microwave on high for 1 minute or until melted.

Step 3: MAKE EGG MIXTURE

Mix together the eggs, remaining milk, chicken, and half of the onion in a small bowl. Place the butter in a large skillet over medium high heat. Pour the egg mixture into the skillet. Cook, stirring occasionally, for 3 to 4 minutes or until the eggs are just set, but not dry.

Step 4: ASSEMBLE SANDWICHES

Place a heaping spoonful of egg and chicken mixture onto each bagel half. Drizzle with a spoonful of cheese sauce and sprinkle with the remaining onion. Serve hot.

• MAKES 2-3 SERVINGS •

Country Club Scrambled Eggs

Scrambled eggs go uptown with this quick recipe.

4	large eggs
¼	cups heavy cream
½	cup diced rotisserie chicken
2	green onions, sliced, divided
¼	cup cooked bacon pieces
½	teaspoon paprika
½	teaspoon garlic powder
	Pinch ground pepper
1	tablespoon canola oil
1	tablespoon butter
6	frozen puff pastry shells, baked according to package instructions
1	cup shredded Cheddar cheese

Step 1: MIX EGGS

Beat together the eggs, cream, chicken, 1 onion, bacon, paprika, garlic powder, and pepper in a medium bowl.

Step 2: COOK EGGS

Place the oil and butter in a large skillet over medium high heat; pour in the egg mixture. Cook, stirring frequently, for 2 to 3 minutes or until the eggs are just set, but not dry.

Step 3: ASSEMBLE AND SERVE

Place the puff pastry shells on a heat proof serving platter. Divide the egg mixture between the shells; sprinkle with cheese. Place under a broiler for 1 to 2 minutes, just to melt the cheese. Sprinkle with the remaining green onion and serve.

COOKS NOTES: Served with a fresh fruit salad, this makes a terrific brunch or light luncheon.

• MAKES 6 SERVINGS •

Cheddar Chicken and Potato Skillet

Melted Cheddar cheese forms a warm and delicious blanket over crispy potatoes and savory chicken in this rustic breakfast.

2	tablespoons butter
3	tablespoons canola oil
1	cup frozen bell pepper and onion mix, thawed
4	cups frozen Southern style hash brown potatoes, thawed
1	teaspoon ground cumin
2	teaspoons minced garlic
2	cups diced rotisserie chicken
	Kosher salt to taste
	Ground black pepper to taste
6	large eggs
2	cups shredded Cheddar cheese
2	tablespoons chopped fresh cilantro

Step 1: COOK VEGETABLES

Place the butter and oil in a large oven-safe skillet over medium high heat; add the bell pepper mix, hash browns, and cumin. Stir together, and then cook without stirring for 4 to 6 minutes or until brown and crisp on the bottom. Turn over and cook without stirring for another 4 to 6 minutes or until brown and crisp.

Step 2: ADD CHICKEN

Stir the garlic and chicken into the vegetables. Cook until heated through. Check the seasoning, adding salt and pepper as needed.

Step 3: ADD EGGS

Using the back of a small ladle or cup, press 6 evenly spaced indentions into the potato mixture. Crack 1 egg into each hole. Cover and cook for 1 minute, or until the egg is beginning to set.

Step 4: FINISH AND SERVE

Sprinkle with Cheddar cheese and place under the broiler; broil until the cheese is melted and begins to brown. Sprinkle with cilantro and serve.

• MAKES 4-6 SERVINGS •

Loaded Hash Browns

These hash browns will take center stage rather than being relegated to a supporting role at your next breakfast.

½	cup all-purpose flour
⅓	cup yellow cornmeal
1	teaspoon kosher salt
½	teaspoon cayenne pepper
1	teaspoon baking powder
⅓	cup canola oil, plus more for cooking
2	eggs, beaten
4	cups frozen shredded hash brown potatoes, thawed
1	cup frozen diced onions
2	cups diced rotisserie chicken
½	cup cooked bacon pieces
	Canola oil
1	cup sour cream
1	green onion, thinly sliced

Step 1: PREHEAT OVEN

Preheat the oven to 200° F.

Step 2: MIX DRY INGREDIENTS

Mix together the flour, cornmeal, cayenne pepper, salt, and pepper in a medium bowl.

Step 3: MIX WET INGREDIENTS AND VEGETABLES

Beat together oil and eggs in a large mixing bowl. Stir in the hash browns, onion, chicken and bacon.

Step 4: COMBINE DRY AND WET INGREDIENTS

Sprinkle the dry ingredients on top of the wet ingredients; stir to combine.

Step 5: COOK HASH BROWNS

Pour enough canola oil to coat the bottom of a large heavy skillet over medium heat. Scoop about ½ cup of hash brown mixture into the pan; flatten slightly. Cook for 3 to 4 minutes or until golden brown. Flip over and continue to cook for an additional 3 to 4 minutes or until golden. Place on a baking sheet, sprinkle with salt. Keep warm in the preheated oven while cooking the remaining hash browns.

Step 6: GARNISH AND SERVE

Place the hash browns on a serving platter. Garnish with sour cream and sprinkle with green onions. Serve hot.

• MAKES 8-10 SERVINGS •

Index

S

Moo Shu Chicken Burritos, 135

Orange-Ginger Sesame Chicken Rice
    Bowl, 172

Red Curry Chicken Turnovers, 134

Red Curry Pineapple Chicken with Rice,
    180

Sesame Chicken Slaw, 99

Spicy Chicken Broccolini Lo-Mein, 181

Thai Chicken Burritos, 136

Thai Chicken Cabbage Salad with Peanut
    Dressing, 93

sesame seeds

    Chayote-Chicken Asparagus Salad with
        Plum Dressing, 101

    Chinese Chicken Baked Buns, 26

    Edamame-Chicken Cold Rice Salad, 97

    Korean-Style Chicken Wraps, 129

    Orange-Ginger Sesame Chicken Rice
        Bowl, 172

    Plum Chicken Baked Buns, 127

    Red Curry Chicken Turnovers, 134

    Sesame Chicken Slaw, 99

    Spicy Chicken Broccolini Lo-Mein, 181

    Teriyaki Chicken DIY Handrolls, 22

    Thai Chicken Cucumber Cups, 27

shrimp

    Creole Chicken and Shrimp Stew, 65

    Emperor's Fried Rice, 160

sofrito

    Baked Creamy Chicken Sofrito Penne, 187

    Sofrito Chicken Manchego Quesadillas,
        119

sour cream

    Baked Chicken Ziti, 191

    Chicken and Potato Casserole, 193

    Creamy Chicken and Green Bean
        Casserole, 212

    Creamy Chicken and Pea Salad, 86

    Enchilada Stuffed Hash Browns, 240

    Fiesta Chicken Layered Dip, 46

Hot Artichoke-Chicken Dip, 36

Minute Stroganoff with Chicken, 183

Quick Chicken Paprikash, 173

Tarragon Chicken Omelet with Havarti,
    236

South American Chicken Soup, 57

Southern Style BBQ Chicken Mini Corn
    Muffin Bites, 39

Southwest Style Chicken and Corn Chowder,
    64

soy sauce

    Chicken Egg Foo Young Casserole, 210

    Chicken Lo Mein Soup, 67

    Chicken Vegetable Soup with Udon
        Noodles, 61

    Edamame-Chicken Cold Rice Salad, 97

    Emperor's Fried Rice, 160

    Hot and Sour Chicken Soup, 80

    Mandarin Chicken Salad, 98

    Spicy Chicken Broccolini Lo-Mein, 181

    Steamed Egg Cups with Chicken and
        Enoki, 229

    Thai Chicken Burritos, 136

spaghetti, one-pot chicken, 170

special sauce, reuben-style chicken sand-
    wiches with, 114

Spicy Chicken Broccolini Lo-Mein, 181

spinach

    Baked Orzo with Chicken and Spinach,
        206

    Chicken Enchilada Suiza Casserole, 220

    Chicken Florentine Cups with Lemon-
        Thyme Mascarpone, 40

    Chicken Florentine Quiche, 228

    Chicken Florentine Sandwiches, 117

    Chicken-Boursin Stuffed Pasta Shells, 158

    Green Curry Chicken Casserole, 200

    Green Curry Chicken Potstickers with
        Dipping Sauce, 18

    Green Curry Chicken Soup, 73

    Hoisin Chicken Summer Rolls, 28